EASY W
GARDENS

Alison R. Francis

TIME LIFE BOOKS

Alexandria, Virginia

TIME® LIFE BOOKS

Time-Life Books is a division of Time Life Inc.

TIME LIFE INC.
CHAIRMAN AND CEO JIM NELSON
PRESIDENT AND COO STEVEN L. JANAS

TIME-LIFE TRADE PUBLISHING
VICE PRESIDENT AND PUBLISHER NEIL LEVIN
SENIOR DIRECTOR OF ACQUISITIONS AND EDITORIAL RESOURCES JENNIFER PEARCE
DIRECTOR OF NEW PRODUCT DEVELOPMENT CAROLYN CLARK
DIRECTOR OF TRADE SALES DANA HOBSON
DIRECTOR OF MARKETING INGER FORLAND
DIRECTOR OF CUSTOM PUBLISHING JOHN LALOR
DIRECTOR OF SPECIAL MARKETS ROBERT LOMBARDI
DIRECTOR OF DESIGN KATE L. MCCONNELL
PROJECT MANAGER JENNIE HALFANT
COVER DESIGN JODY BILLERT

Originated in Singapore by Master Image
Printed and bound in China by Excel Printing

10 9 8 7 6 5 4 3 2 1

ISBN 0-7370-1153-X

Library of Congress Cataloging-in-Publication Data
The Library of Congress has catalogued the trade version of this title as follows:
Francis, Alison, 1957 -
Easy water gardens / Alison Francis.
p. cm. -- (Time-Life garden factfile)
ISBN 0-7370-0608-0 (spiral binding : alk. paper)
1. Water gardens. I. Title. II. Series.

SB423 .F7 2000
635.9'674--dc21 99-040072

A Marshall Edition
Produced for Marshall Editions by PAGE*One*, Cairn House, Elgiva Lane, Chesham, Buckinghamshire, HP5 2JD

For PAGEOne
Art Director Bob Gordon
Editorial Director Helen Parker
Art Editors Melanie McDowell, Suzanne Tuhrim
Editor Charlotte Stock
Picture Research Nadine Bazar
Photography Peter Anderson, Steve Wooster
Illustrations Karen Gavin

FOR MARSHALL EDITIONS
Managing Editor Anne Yelland
Managing Art Editor Helen Spencer
Editorial Director Ellen Dupont
Art Director Dave Goodman
Editorial Coordinator Ros Highstead
Production Nikki Ingram, Anna Pauletti
DTP Lesley Gilbert

Measurements are given in imperial, followed by the metric equivalent in parentheses. Use one or the other when doing work, as the two measurements are not exactly equivalent.

Contents

INTRODUCTION

The sight and sound of water will bring a feeling of tranquillity to even the busiest and noisiest of gardens. Visitors, both young and old, will always head straight for the pond, while animals, butterflies, birds, and insects are all drawn to even the simplest of water features. Anyone can have a water feature to suit their space and budget – from a mini-pond in a barrel on a balcony to a more ambitious project, complete with plants and fish, fountain, and lights. Once built and stocked, a pond or water feature needs very little looking after, so you really can sit back and enjoy it.

CREATING A WATER GARDEN

This book is designed to help you create your own perfect water garden, whatever its size, shape, and style. Whether you are a total novice or an experienced water gardener the advice given here on the materials and techniques that you will need to construct different types of ponds and water features, plus tips on the best plants and fish to choose, will help you to avoid some of the pitfalls of water gardening.

Before you rush out to buy a pond, fish, and plants, take time to think carefully about what it is you really want from a water feature and how much space and time you have. If you opt for a pond in favor of a smaller water feature, Chapter 1 looks at where a pond might best be sited in your garden; the merits of formal and informal designs; the pros and cons of a sunken pond versus a raised one; the choice of liners available; and how deep a pond needs to be. Essential guidance is given on general safety.

Building a pond

Work begins in Chapter 2 as the building of a pond gets under way. But even this has been made a whole lot easier with the introduction of rigid preformed shells and flexible liners. The hardest part is digging the hole! Together with the tools and materials needed, simple step-by-step instructions will enable you to construct a pond in a weekend. The whole thing can be stocked and up and running in just a few more days.

The five main groups of aquatic plants are looked at in detail, together with advice on their planting, feeding, and general care. No feature in a garden can be so relied upon to induce a feeling of relaxation as a pond reflecting sunlight, while the sound of water splashing over a cascade or from a fountain instantly cools a hot summer's day. Lighting can effect a magical transformation as dusk falls. To further enhance the enjoyment of your water feature, why not add a fountain or some lights? Pond hardware – from pumps and filters to fountains, waterfalls, and lights – are reviewed along with some suggestions for ornaments and statues.

Small water features

You don't even need a garden to have a pond. Chapter 3 looks at different ways of creating a simple mini-pond in a half-barrel and old sink. Tips and advice are also given on the plants to choose for your miniature water feature, including a selection of dwarf waterlilies. Other ideas include birdbaths, wall-mounted and free-standing fountains, a pebble pool, and a millstone bubble feature. Simple instructions are given showing how to install a pebble pool and how to create a miniature pumped feature from a simple kit.

Life in the pond

There is a simple but enormously satisfying pleasure in keeping fish. And there's an even greater thrill when a frog or toad takes up residence, or you spot your first dragonfly. Chapter 4 takes a look at how to provide the perfect habitat for both fish and other wildlife.

Keeping ornamental fish is a simple matter, provided a few basic rules are obeyed, which are given here, along with a selection of fish suitable for a garden pond and tips on how to recognize problems. If you are interested in wildlife, details are given on features to include in a wildlife pond – and on the special conditions needed for growing bog plants. Information is given on what creatures you can expect to take up residence in your pond, and how to create the right habitat to attract and keep them. There is also advice on humane ways of deterring unwelcome visitors such as herons and cats.

Pond care and maintenance

Having built your pond or water feature and got it up and running, planted, and stocked with fish, you'll need to take care of it. Chapter 5 deals with the general care and maintenance of a garden pond, starting with the tools and equipment you will need and moving on to some of the more fundamental tasks that you will have to undertake when necessary, such as draining and cleaning the pond.

Throughout the year, season by season, there are routine jobs you can do to maintain a balance in the pond, such as removing blanketweed in spring and summer and skimming off debris in the fall. Depending on the severity of the winter in the area in which you live, there are also a number of tasks you will need to undertake to prepare the pond for the cold weather – these may range from completely closing down and destocking the pond to preventing the pond from icing over.

The troubleshooter's guide to what can go wrong with plants, fish, and water may look a little daunting at first, but few troubles ail a garden pond, so treat this guide as simply a reference to what may go wrong, not what will go wrong.

Plant directory

No one can fail to be impressed by the serenity and beauty of a waterlily and its dazzling waxy flowers in summer, while stately irises with their dramatic foliage rise majestically above the surface from submerged roots. Plants in and around a pond will add a new dimension to your garden, as they will grow there and nowhere else. Chapter 6 provides a directory of suitable plants for a garden pond.

Many plants perform a vital role, such as the fully submerged oxygenators that help keep a pond clean and healthy, or floating aquatics that shade the surface of the water. Marginals, on the other hand, are purely for our pleasure, whether it is their flowers, foliage, or both that are their main attraction. These should be planted in groups of the same variety, rather than singly, for maximum impact.

One square yard (square meter) of space is ample for a few oxygenators, a marginal plant or two, a waterlily or other floater, and a couple of medium-sized fish. The greater the surface area the more plants you can have – but don't be tempted to overplant, you still want to see some water and its inhabitants. And don't forget the area around the pond can be turned into a bog garden – there is a list of suggestions for plant varieties that are happy in the permanently moist conditions that are found there.

Happy water gardening!

1

Creating a water garden

CREATING A WATER GARDEN

The sight and sound of moving water and the living beauty of plants and fish will add a new dimension to your garden, and to your overall enjoyment of it.

A garden pond, whether formal, informal, or completely natural, and whatever its size, will also encourage wildlife, and so in a small way you will be providing a little sanctuary for nature in your own garden.

This chapter of the book looks at the basics of creating a pond: where it should go, how big you should make it, and the choices to be made between a formal or informal design, and whether it should be sunken or raised. Then there is a decision to be made about materials for its construction. Finally, there's the all-important question of creating, and maintaining, a healthy balance in the pond.

INTRODUCING WATER

No garden, whatever its size or style, can ever be complete without some kind of water feature to add life and movement. Even if you do not have enough space for a pond, many garden centers stock a wide range of simple, easy-to-construct water features to suit even the smallest garden. Alternatively, a pond will breathe new life into a neglected corner of a larger, more established garden.

CONSIDER THE OPTIONS

Before deciding on a water feature for your garden, first take a trip to your local water garden center or browse through a mail-order catalog – you'll find plenty of choices when it comes to flexible liners and ready-made ponds in all shapes and sizes. You'll also find the materials to construct waterfalls and cascades, as well as self-contained water features, and an impressive selection of pumps, fountains, and lights.

The wide range of materials and equipment available is designed to bring pond-making within the scope of any handy gardener. Before you part with any money, however, make sure you have the answers to the few questions in the box below.

And don't forget those optional extras – fountains, waterfalls, and lights. Provision will need to be made for electricity to be run to these features if they are to be installed.

POINTS TO CONSIDER

- How much space is available?
- Where is the best place for a pond or water feature in your garden?
- What type of pond do you want?
- Plants and fish – do you want both?
- Is wildlife important to you?

A SOLUTION FOR LIMITED SPACE

PONDS WITH A PURPOSE

■ **Patio focus** A sunken or partially raised pond on a patio forms a focal point, attracting people to linger, their senses soothed by the limpid water, and the seemingly effortless movement of fish.

■ **Lawn feature** A formal pond with waterlilies and a fountain makes an eye-catching feature set within a landscaped lawn.

■ **Wildlife haven** A natural pond, rich in native plants provides a home for frogs, toads, and newts, as well as attracting dragonflies and other insects, which in turn attract birds.

LIMITED SPACE?

If space is really tight, a mini-pond can be created in a half-barrel, deep sink, or small rigid liner, and this will provide a home for a range of aquatic plants (see Chapter 3). In cool climates, where winter temperatures drop below freezing, small features may freeze solid and will need to be dismantled seasonally at the onset of cold weather.

Self-contained water features such as pebble ponds take up little space and recycle the water – a bonus in arid areas and times of drought.

CAREFUL PLANNING

A carefully planned garden pond that is well built, stocked, and cared for provides a constant source of enjoyment. Take care at the planning stage to address the following points, all of which are covered in detail within the pages of this book:

- **Position** Make sure you choose the right location for the pond.

- **Size** Take care that you build the pond to the optimum size and proportions.

- **Planting** Choosing the right type of plants is vital to the well-being of the pond and its contents – not all will necessarily be decorative.

GRAND DESIGNS
A formal pond combined with modern architectural structures adds depth and reflection to a traditional garden setting.

POSITION AND SIZE

More important than the style of a pond, whether it be formal or informal, sunken or raised, are its position in the garden and its size in relation to the range of fish and water plants you may want to introduce. Unlike most other features in a garden, once a pond has been installed, it will be very difficult to move!

CLOSE TO THE HOUSE

For maximum enjoyment, unless you have a very large garden, the best position for a pond, or water feature, is as near to the house as possible, so that it can be seen from the windows. Also, from a practical point of view, if you plan to have a fountain, waterfall, or lights, it will be easy to run electricity to the pond.

The pond should also be near a path. Not only will this make the construction of it easier, but a path leading from the house to the water feature will encourage you to visit it more often. Once planted up and stocked with fish, you will want to have easy access to it, so position your pond where it can be viewed at all times of the day...and year!

THE RIGHT SPOT FOR A POND

- Visible from windows in the house.
- Easily accessible via a path leading from the house.
- In the sun for part of the day.
- Away from overhanging trees, particularly those that lose their leaves, blossoms, or fruit.
- Out of the shade of nearby buildings and walls.
- Sheltered from prevailing winds.
- As near as practical to a source of electricity for operating a fountain, waterfall, or lights.

MOVABLE STONE TROUGH FOUNTAIN

Decorative cobbles conceal pump equipment

AN OPEN SITUATION

An open situation is essential for pond life, as neither aquatic plants nor fish will thrive in deep shade, while the scourge of all pond keepers, green algae, will flourish, making the water uninhabitable.

Fish cannot tolerate the pollution caused by leaves and other vegetation that fall into the water, so keep the pond away from deciduous trees or those that shed berries or blossoms.

IDEAL SETTING
A summerhouse looks down over an informal pond. The trees are set back and the lush planting tiered to allow light to reach the water's surface.

SHELTERED FROM WIND

Make sure the spot you choose provides some shelter from prevailing winds – in spring, to prevent young foliage being scorched, and later in the season to guard against taller marginals being blown over. Waterlilies in particular are affected by wind ruffling the water's surface.

One way to provide shelter is to build up a rock garden beside the pond, using soil from the excavated hole, or plant a hedge of conifers, which do not shed their leaves.

If the pond is to be sunk into the ground, the site needs to be level. However, if the only suitable site is sloping, it would be better to build a raised pond. Avoid siting your pond in an area that is badly drained and prone to waterlogging. Although moisture-loving plants will thrive, a pond liable to flooding will be difficult to manage and maintain.

LET THE SUN SHINE IN

It is important to site the pond where the sun will shine on it for at least part of the day. Apart from the pleasure sitting in the sun gives us, there are practical advantages. Waterlilies, for instance, need sun: they appreciate at least 10–12 hours a day in the height of summer. Fish, too, will benefit from the warmth, although they are sensitive to rapid changes in temperature. This is why they need some shade, such as that provided beneath waterlily leaves and other floating aquatics. These plants will flourish in such a sunny spot and, in turn, will provide plenty of surface shade for the fish.

OUT IN THE OPEN
An informal pond in an open position supports a wide range of aquatic and marginal plants and fish and provides an attractive feature in an area of lawn.

MOVING WATER
The refreshing sound of a gently splashing fountain brings life and movement to an otherwise static formal feature.

STAYING CLEAR OF TREES

Few things are more lethal to the inhabitants of a garden pond than decaying leaves. As they slowly decompose, they give off gases that can be harmful to fish and are of no benefit to plants. The pond can deal with its own decaying matter, but a sudden influx of any "foreign" leaves will upset the natural balance, leading to an excess of methane gas – the main reason for an increase in fatalities among fish during the winter months.

THE SOURCE OF POWER

The proximity to an electrical connection is important. If you plan to have a fountain or waterfall, you will need a pump and electricity to operate them. Likewise, if you want to illuminate your pond or water feature after dark, there needs to be a power source close by.

If possible, the power outlet should be installed inside the house or in a conservatory to avoid having to go out at night or in inclement weather should the need arise. If not, it should be in a garage or nearby shed.

Although pond pumps, fountains, and lights are usually low voltage, wherever electricity is being used in the garden, always use a residual current circuit breaker (RCCB), or power-breaker unit, which will trip and cut off the current immediately if anything goes wrong (see p. 17).

Warning

- Avoid planting laburnum and laurel close to the pond as both have toxic seeds as well as leaves.
- Keep cherry and plum trees away from the water as they are host to the waterlily aphid (see p. 90).
- While it might be tempting to have a weeping tree by the side of your pond, think again! Tree roots, such as those of the willow, may undermine and damage the fabric of the pond.

WHY SIZE MATTERS

The success of a pond relies on a balance of fish, insect, and plant life so, within reason, always aim to make your pond as large – in terms of water surface area – as you can. If space permits, the minimum size recommended to gain the right conditions for clear water and the necessary balance is a surface area of 40 sq ft (3.7 sq m), equal to a pond measuring 8 ft x 5 ft (2.4 m x 1.5 m). A large pond is easier to manage than a small one, just make sure that it blends with the rest of the garden.

RIGHT DEPTH FOR PLANTS

A garden pond need not be very deep: many aquatic plants will be happy in no more than 18 in (45 cm) of water. Marginal plants, which have their roots in the water but their leaves and flowers out in the open air, will need a shelf on which to stand their pots. This shelf must be about 9 in (22 cm) below the surface of the water and 9–12 in (22–30 cm) wide, and can run all, or just part of the way around the pond. This will accommodate a 6-in (15-cm)-deep plant container, leaving 3 in (7.5 cm) of water over the top of it. Most marginals are grown at this depth. Where plants require shallower water, their pot or container can be raised to the desired level by standing it on paving stones or bricks.

RIGHT DEPTH FOR FISH

If you plan to keep fish, goldfish will survive quite happily in a depth of 18–24 in (45–60 cm). Koi, on the other hand, need the water to be at least 3 ft (1 m) deep, as they can grow several feet long.

The deeper the pond, the safer the fish will be during a cold winter as the water should not freeze all the way to the bottom. Neither fish nor plants like sudden and frequent changes in temperature, which are common occurences in small ponds both in winter and in summer. The greater the volume of water the more constant the temperature will be within it. Whatever the size of pond you choose for your garden, the overriding factor to keep in mind is proportion.

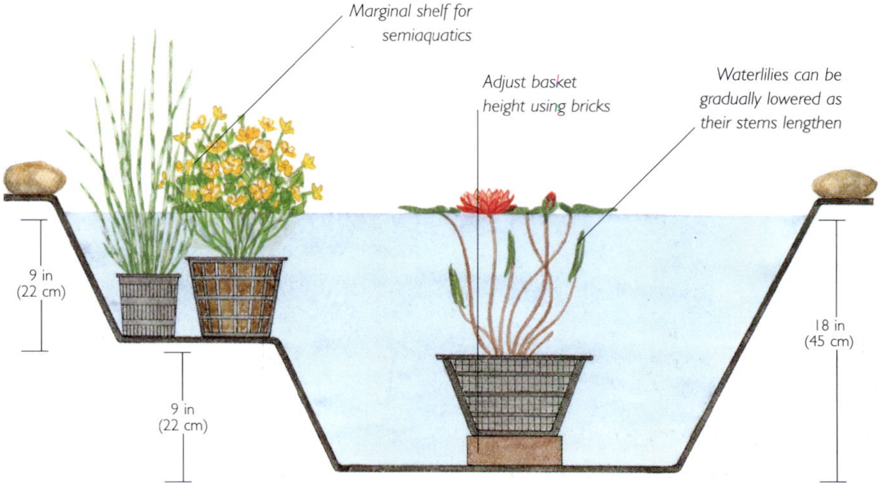

SAFETY FIRST

When planning a water feature, always consider safety, particularly if the garden is used by young children, older people, or domestic pets. You will also need to pay careful attention to electrical installations – water and electricity can be a fatal combination.

SAFETY FOR CHILDREN

Water, even just a couple of inches, can be lethal to small children, yet it is like a magnet to them, particularly crawling babies and toddlers.

■ **Mini-features** In preference to a pond, consider a small water feature, such as a mini-pool or bubble fountain (see Chapter 3) that has no open surface of water.

■ **Out of bounds** If you want to include a pond in your garden make sure it is inaccessible to children who play there, unless there is an adult around to supervise at all times.

■ **Pond alternatives** While children are young, a raised pond can be converted into a raised bed for flowers and shrubs until they grow older. Similarly, a sunken pond can be filled in with sand to make an ideal sandbox.

ELECTRICAL SAFETY TIPS

- Check that all electrical equipment is safety approved for outdoor use.
- Switch off and disconnect electrical equipment before handling.
- Make sure that all cabling and connectors are waterproof.
- Always use a power-breaker/RCCB when using electricity outdoors.

Warning

If you sink a pond into a patio take measures to ensure that there is no possibility of anyone, young or old, tripping and falling in.

ELECTRICAL SAFETY

Electricity in the garden is a potential hazard. Low-voltage lighting and pumps for small water features are available in simple kit form and can be installed by an amateur. These work in conjunction with a transformer that reduces the voltage from the house making it safe. Place the transformer indoors as close to the wall socket as possible.

■ Make sure you always follow the manufacturer's instructions and, if in doubt, hire a qualified electrician to double-check your wiring – or even to do it for you.

■ Ask a qualified electrician to connect you to the electrical supply.

■ Once installed, all equipment must be properly maintained and serviced.

■ To prevent accidents, all cabling must be buried and protected by an armored steel casing.

■ Larger fountains and waterfalls require high-voltage electricity and should be installed by a professional.

DESIGN IDEAS

A pond or water feature will create an area of cool reflection in most gardens, whatever the size or style. Although very much a matter of personal preference, when it comes to deciding the style and shape of your pond, consider the position in which you intend to locate it. The two basic styles of a pond are formal and informal.

THE FORMAL APPROACH

Close to a building or within an area of paving, it is advisable to opt for a more formal style of a pond. A strict geometric shape – square, rectangular, oval, or circular – will link the pond with the lines of any hard landscaping close by.

In an ultramodern garden, you could consider more complex but still regular shapes, such as a triangular pond. Although formal ponds tend to be built at ground level, there is no reason why they should not be raised.

FORMAL FOCUS
A small, circular, mosaic-lined pond and stream become a focal point in this Mediterranean-style garden, helping to break up the monotony of a large paved area.

FORMAL TIPS

- Site a formal pond where it will reflect nearby objects, such as trees, a statue, or just open sky.
- Consider introducing a small fountain and underwater lighting to give added effect, especially on summer evenings.
- Avoid marginals, which may obscure the clearly defined outline of the pond. If needed, a carefully positioned container may add a degree of softness.
- An edging of paving stones or bricks makes a formal pond perfect for a patio.

A MORE INFORMAL STYLE

Away from the strictures of hard landscaping, you can adopt a more informal style, perhaps mirroring the natural curves of a lawn or border. As the outline of an informal pond is irregular and not so clearly defined, it will look more like a natural water feature, making it ideal if you want to encourage wildlife into your pond and garden.

When deciding on an informal style, bear in mind that its construction and maintenance will take slightly more effort than a formal pond. Acquiring a more "natural" look takes time and patience.

INFORMAL TIPS

- A molded liner will give your pond a predetermined shape. A flexible liner offers more creative scope, but keep your design simple – this will make it easier to construct and the final effect will look more natural.
- Soften the outline of the pond with a selection of marginal plants or a bog garden (see pp. 76–77). Marginal plantings look most effective if they appear to flow down into the water.
- Do not allow grass to grow right up to the pond's edges otherwise mowing will be awkward to carry out and clippings will have to be removed from the surface of the water before they sink and rot.

INFORMAL CASCADE
Gently trickling cascades and a decorative fountain combine with lush exotic foliage to add height and atmosphere to a partly shaded corner of a tropical-style garden.

PLANNING YOUR POND

Once you have decided on either a formal or informal pond, you need to choose whether it should be raised or sunken. Both kinds have their advantages depending on position, climate, and your own particular circumstances, but in the end it comes down to personal choice. Whatever style and shape of pond you settle on, however, before you start digging any holes, write your ideas down on paper.

RAISED OR SUNKEN?

Although there are exceptions, as a general rule a raised pond lends itself to a more formal style, while a sunken pond is more suited to an informal or wildlife setting. The list below highlights some advantages and disadvantages of each.

Most well-equipped pond and garden centers stock a wide range of pond liners (see pp. 22–25), which can be used for both types of pond.

RAISED TIMBER POND

RAISED VERSUS SUNKEN – THE PROS AND CONS

RAISED OR PARTIALLY RAISED	SUNKEN
• Makes an excellent focal point in a formal garden or on a paved area.	• Resemblance to a natural pond suits an informal or wildlife setting.
• Low surrounding walls can be used as casual seating to observe pond life.	• Can be extended at margins to incorporate a bog garden.
• Best suited to climates where winter temperatures remain above freezing.	• Successful even in cool climates as water below ground level is less likely to freeze solid.
• Walls can be built to varying heights, offering a solution for sloping sites.	• Provides a healthier environment for plants and fish, as the water temperature remains more constant.
• Needs less excavation.	• Less expensive to build because there is less hard landscaping to consider.
• Maintenance is easier, particularly for the elderly or disabled who may find bending awkward.	• More hazardous for young children and household pets.
• Takes longer to build than a sunken pond and tends to be more expensive.	• Needs excavating. The resultant spoil needs to be removed or reused elsewhere in the garden.
• Surrounding wall prevents children from accidentally falling in the water.	

MAKING PLANS

■ **Sketch your ideas** On a piece of squared paper, sketch a rough plan of your garden, to scale, showing the house, boundaries, and any existing features, including trees and shrubs. This will give you an idea of just how much space you have for a pond.

■ **Make adjustments** Following your plan, mark out the outline of the pond on the ground using a length of rope or garden hose. Leave it in place for a few days so you can view it from outdoors and indoors at different times of the day. Notice where shadows fall as the sun moves and if the pond is going to be too shady adjust the design as necessary.

■ **Think ahead** Allow space around the pond for paving or plants – perhaps even a bog garden. Don't forget to include a place to sit by the side of the pond so that once the building work is finished, you can sit and enjoy the wildlife, plants, and fish on a summer's evening.

EXAMPLE OF A GARDEN PLAN
Each square on the plan below represents 3 sq ft (1 sq m). The pond has been positioned close to the house in an open, sunny area.

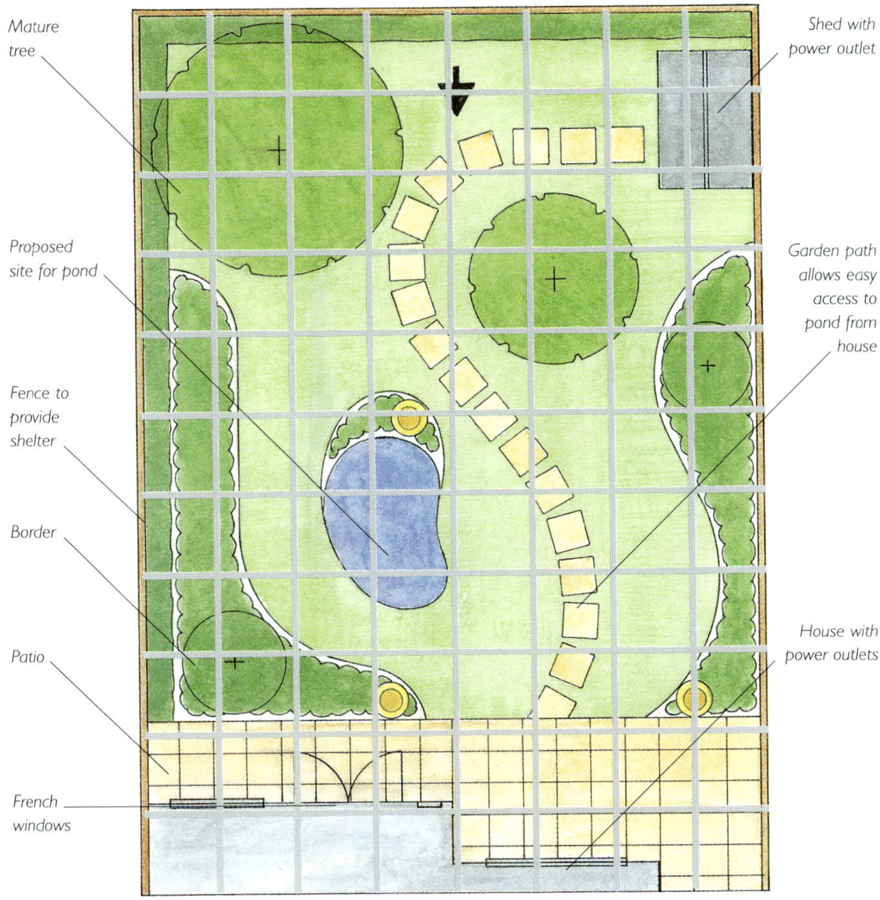

MATERIALS

When it comes to building a pond, there is a wide choice of materials available, the most common being flexible sheet liners, rigid preformed liners, and concrete. The welcomed arrival of flexible liners and molded ponds has revolutionized pond construction. Easy to install, a garden pond designed to meet individual needs can be built in a weekend.

FLEXIBLE SHEET LINERS

Versatile and relatively inexpensive, flexible sheet liners can be used to line almost any size and shape of a water feature, with the exception of square and rectangular ponds. Price-wise they are relatively inexpensive and have the added advantage of being easy to take home from the garden center in the car.

Most liners can be bought either "off the roll," which will work out cheaper particularly if you are planning a big project, or in precut packs, which are ideal for a smaller pond.

There are four main types of material used for pond liners, most of which come in different weights and thicknesses. The thicker the material, the more durable it will be, but it will also be more expensive. Whatever the material, however, check that it is "fish-grade," which means it will not give off any harmful chemicals, and that it is UV-stabilized to resist ultraviolet sun damage. It should also carry a 10–20-year guarantee.

■ **Butyl liners** Although more costly, butyl liners are virtually indestructible. Made from a kind of synthetic rubber, they are unaffected by sunlight or frost, and despite being fairly thick, are flexible even in cold weather. Their elasticity makes it possible to lay them with fewer creases and folds than PVC and polyethylene.

■ **EPDM liners** Also made from a durable synthetic rubber, EPDM liners share many of the qualities of butyl.

BUTYL LINER

PVC LINER

■ **PVC** Popular, flexible, and cheaper than butyl and EPDM, PVC liners come in different thicknesses, which is reflected in their prices.

■ **Polyethylene** Although relatively inexpensive, low-density polyethylene, or LDPE, liners will not last as long as other materials. LDPE is stronger and more flexible.

COLOR CODE

Lighter colors reflect too much light, so if the liner you buy has a lighter side, put this face down in the hole. Flexible liners are usually available in a choice of black or green.

■ **Black** A black liner absorbs light and heat and creates an illusion of depth. Fish also show up better.

■ **Green** A green liner absorbs less light than black, so a green liner should help keep algae levels lower.

FLEXIBLE LINERS

ADVANTAGES

- Versatile for use in creative water garden designs as their use is not restricted to a particular size, shape, or depth. Ideal for features such as cascades and streams.
- Ideal for an informal or a natural wildlife pond and bog garden.
- Easy to transport home.
- Can be used to instantly "repair" a leaking concrete or rigid pond.

DISADVANTAGES

- Can be damaged by sharp stones or tree roots if not adequately bedded.
- Marginal shelves have to be built when using a flexible liner.
- Not suited to the angles necessary for a square or rectangular pond.

REPAIRING LEAKS

Basic repair kits can be used to patch all types of liner. Polyethylene liners are not worth repairing.

- Empty the pond and identify the damaged area.
- Thoroughly clean the surrounding area with a scrub brush and water.
- Allow to dry then clean with a cloth wetted with alcohol.
- Place the repair patch over the leak and press firmly.
- Wait at least 12 hours before refilling the pond.

REPAIR PATCH

BEDDING DOWN

A flexible liner is usually bedded on a 1–2-in (2.5–5-cm) layer of damp sand (see Chapter 2 for construction methods). However, as a precaution against punctures, particularly if your soil is stony, it is well worth investing in a polyester matting underlay, which usually comes in rolls.

UNDERLAY

RIGID PREFORMED LINERS

Preformed, molded pond shells are available in a wide range of shapes and sizes, so it is worth shopping around until you find one that matches your requirements. For a formal raised pond on a patio, choose simple, regular shapes, such as circles and rectangles. Irregular outlines are more popular for sunken ponds, and some of these would be almost impossible to create using a flexible liner. Bear in mind that simple shapes are the easiest to excavate and backfill.

Various materials are used in the manufacture of molded liners, including fiberglass and different grades of plastic. A good-quality fiberglass liner should last a lifetime.

■ Check that planting shelves are at least 9 in (22 cm) wide – to take a decent-sized container. If the shelf is too narrow, plants will topple over in the wind or fish will knock them off.

■ Choose a dark color and before you buy, check that the minimum depth is at least 18 in (45 cm), and that it carries a 10-year guarantee.

■ If intending to stock with fish, check that the unit is big and deep enough (see p. 16).

PREFORMED LINERS

ADVANTAGES

- Ideally suited for a formal pond, either sunken or raised, especially within a paved area.
- Easy to install and maintain.
- Marginal shelves are ready formed.

DISADVANTAGES

- Too big to transport home by car.
- Tend to look bigger in a garden center than in your garden.

RESIN-FIBERGLASS

Virtually indestructible, resistant to water, frost, and ultraviolet light, fiberglass liners come preformed in a variety of shapes and can be simply bedded on sand in an excavated hole. They can be expensive, but don't compromise when it comes to size: go for the biggest you can afford and accommodate. A fiberglass pond should come with a 20-year guarantee.

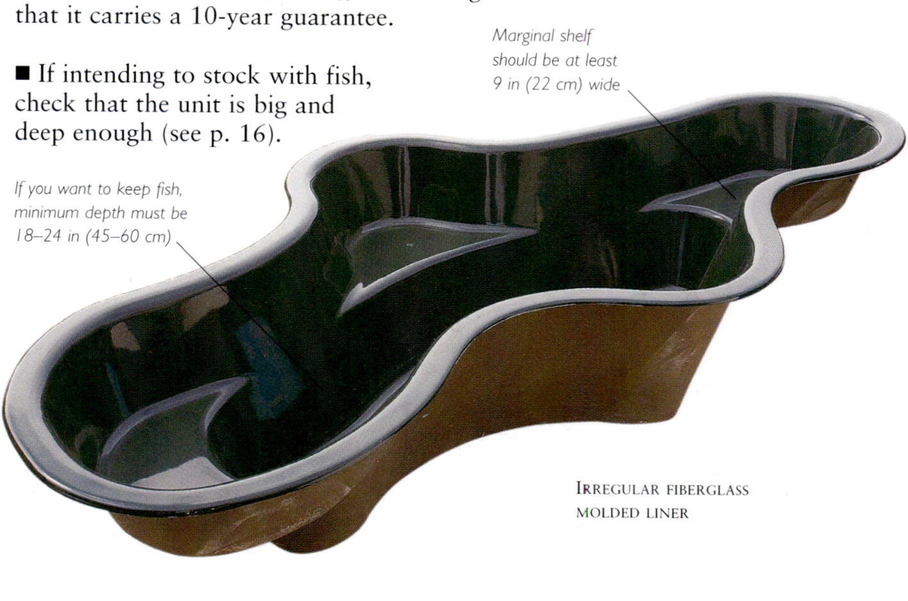

IRREGULAR FIBERGLASS MOLDED LINER

NATURAL STONE-EFFECT ROCK POOL

Fiber-glass is also used for small water features with a naturalistic rock or stone finish that encourages the growth of lichens and algae.

REINFORCED PLASTIC

Molded plastic liners look much the same as fiberglass but are thinner and more brittle. Although cheaper, they have a shorter life expectancy. Choose one with a long guarantee – usually between 10–20 years. Length of guarantee is a good indicator of durability and resistance to light degradation. Sunlight will weaken ordinary plastic liners and the corners will crack with age, so it's important when installing it in your garden to ensure that all of the liner is covered and none is left exposed.

CONCRETE PONDS

Until the appearance of flexible and molded liners, all garden ponds were built using concrete. Concrete ponds do, however, require a certain amount of expertise and their construction is probably best left to a professional.

ADVANTAGES

- Used correctly, concrete makes the strongest and most permanent pond.
- A concrete pond can be any shape or size you wish.

DISADVANTAGES

- Building a concrete pond is difficult and time-consuming, which can make it an expensive project. It is probably best left to professionals.
- Ground movement and freezing temperatures can cause cracks and therefore leaks.
- Raw concrete is harmful to fish. All inside surfaces need to be painted with a sealant before filling with water.

RIGID PLASTIC MOLDED LINER

KEEPING A BALANCE

A successful pond is one in which each of the components – water, plant life, fish, soil, and organic matter – interact as part of a mini-ecosystem. To prevent overcrowding and the water turning green and murky, it is essential to maintain this delicate balance.

GOOD PONDKEEPING

Here's how to create conditions that are suitable for plants and fish but which will keep algae at bay:

■ **Debris** Remove fallen leaves and other debris immediately – if allowed to decay it will pollute the water.

■ **Soil mix** Do not use peat, garden compost, or manure when planting.

■ **Plant oxygenators** Oxygenating plants (see p. 40) keep the water clean by inhibiting algae growth. They also provide oxygen for fish.

■ **Feeding** Do not give fish any more food than they can consume in five minutes. Skim off uneaten food.

■ **Size** If your pond has a surface area of less than 40 sq ft (3.7 sq m) and a depth of less than 18 in (45 cm), you may need to use a filter (see p. 49) or an algicide in the water to stop green algae and protect fish.

SURFACE COVER
The floating leaves of waterlilies and other deep-water aquatics should cover about half the surface to provide some shade for pond life.

Building a pond

BUILDING A POND

All you really need to build your own pond are a little advanced planning, a flick through a mail-order catalog, and a visit to a water garden specialist combined with a few basic tools and materials plus some hard labor.

This chapter takes you through the various methods for constructing your own pond, using either a flexible or rigid liner. Useful tips are given for both sunken and raised ponds. There are ideas for edgings and general information on the range of water plants available and how to plant them. The chapter ends with some creative ideas for bringing movement, light, and ornamentation to your water feature.

Tools and Materials

A simple pond, no more than a couple of feet deep (up to 60 cm), sunk into the ground, is as easy to build as planting a tree – the hardest part is digging the hole! Whether you use a rigid or a flexible liner, this is a project that could easily be tackled over a weekend. A raised pond will need a little more time and effort spent on it.

2

Basic tools

Any task will be made much easier if you have the right tools for it – and in certain situations it is crucial to use the correct equipment. Consider borrowing or renting tools that you might never or rarely need again. If buying, it is well worth investing in good-quality tools if you can. They are usually longer-lasting and more comfortable to use.

■ **Leveling** Mark out the dimensions with a flexible tape measure and use a carpenter's level to ensure the pond is straight. A straightedge, such as a plank, is a useful guide for digging.

■ **Digging the hole** Use a fork and a sharp-edged spade for breaking the soil and a broad shovel for scooping out loose earth. A pickaxe is handy if there are large stones or tree roots to deal with. Remove the excavated soil from the site in a wheelbarrow.

■ **Brick and paving edging** Use a bricklayer's trowel for handling wet building mixes around the edge.

Garden spade and fork

Materials

The basic materials for making a pond, such as sand, mortar, and cement, should all be available from a good builders' supply store. Water garden specialists will stock a wide range of liners and underlay (see pp. 22–25).

If you are constructing a raised pool with a brick wall surround and decorative stone edging, make a trip to a local builders' supply store. Go armed with the length, height, and width of the walls for your pond, and ask them to help you work out what you'll need in terms of bricks and mortar. If the pond is going on an existing patio, try to choose materials in the same range. It is a good idea to take along a sample of the patio paving with you to be sure of a good match. If you don't have this, a photograph is the next best thing.

Don't forget coping stones for capping the walls. These will keep out damp, dirt, and debris and hide away any electrical cables for lights and fountains. Many well-stocked landscape gardening centers offer a good range of suitable stones. If you are planning to use the pond edge as a comfortable place to sit, make sure you select stones that are wide and flat enough.

WATER VOLUME

Use the following simple formulas to calculate the volume of water you will require to fill your pond. The measurements are given in imperial with metric in parentheses.

RECTANGULAR PONDS
Volume in gallons (liters) = average length in ft (m) x average width in ft (m) x average depth in ft (m) x 6.2 (1,000).

CIRCULAR PONDS
Volume in gallons (liters) = 3.14 x ½ diameter in ft (m) x ½ diameter in ft (m) x depth in ft (m) x 6.2 (1,000).

WHY YOU NEED A PUMP...

An electric pump (see p. 48) is essential for moving water in features such as fountains and cascades. The movement it creates also helps maintain oxygen levels, which is particularly important in hot, sultry weather. Pumps are also used for circulating water through filtration systems. All pumps require electricity to be brought to the pond.

AND MAYBE A FILTER

A pond filter (see p. 49) helps keep the pond water clean and healthy. Mechanical filters strain out solid particles, while biological filters use materials with large, complex surface areas on which bacteria collect and flourish to break down and purify waste products in the water. An ultraviolet purifier is an effective means of keeping algae at bay.

LINER QUANTITY

The following simple calculations will enable you to work out the approximate size of flexible liner you will require for a sunken pond, regardless of the shape of the pond and size of the marginal shelves.

Length of liner = the overall length of pond + twice the maximum depth.

Width of liner = the overall width of pond + twice the maximum depth.

OTHER ACCESSORIES

When it comes to stocking your finished pond with plants, you will eventually also need a range of suitable planting baskets and containers (see pp. 42–43) as well as the plants themselves.

If you want to shed a little light on your water feature, most water garden specialists stock a good range to choose from, including lights that can be submerged in the water (see pp. 50–51).

Finally, why not complete the effect with a pondside ornament (see p. 52).

USING A FLEXIBLE LINER

Flexible sheet liner is the most versatile material available to water gardeners as it offers none of the restrictions of size and shape that accompany rigid preformed liners. Use it to line containers of almost any size and shape to create your own innovative and original water features, or to renew the life of an old leaking pond by simply adding a new lining on top of the old. It really comes into its own for constructing informal sunken ponds – and as you become more adventurous, try experimenting with free-form streams and cascades.

2

SOLID GROUND

Flexible liner can be used to line almost any water feature, however complex. Its flexibility means it can even be laid over hard ground, as long as the site is properly prepared beforehand. Most important, always remove any sharp stones and roots and lay the liner on a 1-in (2.5-cm) layer of damp sand covered with synthetic underlay.

AVOIDING WASTAGE

To avoid wastage, it is advisable to excavate more complex water features and make any necessary amendments to the design before buying the liner. In this way, if you decide to make a part of the design bigger, you will not be stuck with the quantity and dimensions of liner you bought to construct your feature to the original plan.

FLEXIBLE-LINED WATERCOURSE

Extending planting around the pond

Although many rigid preformed liners now incorporate varying depths of water to suit different plants, they cannot compete with the versatility of a flexible liner. When constructing your pond, try varying the depth around the edges to create pockets of moisture.

By extending the area of liner around the edges of the pond at the construction stage, rather than trimming it back, you can use your imagination to create bog gardens (see pp. 76–77), stony beaches, and islands. Once they have been planted up, not only will these features disguise the edges of your pond, making it almost indistinguishable from a natural pond, they will also give access to a variety of wildlife.

If the flexible liner is buried beneath the soil at the water's edge, even if it is above the water level, plants in the surrounding soil will draw moisture from the pond. In small areas, this is acceptable; however, unless a large bog garden is made independent of the pond, the plants will quickly deplete the level of water in the pond. To prevent water from seeping out of the pond, allow the liner to come up out of the ground and mortar rocks or pavers on top of it.

PRACTICAL TIPS FOR USING A FLEXIBLE LINER

- The sides of a sunken pond need to slope at about 20° to prevent soil collapse during digging and to allow the liner to stretch without too many creases. It will also allow a sheet of ice to float upward without damaging the liner. You can judge the angle of slope by measuring 3 in (7.5 cm) inward for every 9 in (22 cm) of depth. If the soil is very sandy, increase the angle of slope for extra stability.

- Be careful to remove any sharp stones and tree roots from the area where you are planning to use your flexible liner, or these will cause a puncture. Repair kits (see p. 23) are available if the liner is damaged, but patching will weaken the liner. Prolong the lifespan of flexible liner by using a special underliner to cushion and protect it.

- If soil is very stony, cover it with a layer of damp, fine sand to a depth of 1–2 in (2.5–5 cm). Gently tread the base down, then rake it.

- Plan projects using flexible liner for a warm, sunny day. If you leave the liner in position in the sun for a couple of hours it will become more pliable and enable you to avoid excessive creasing.

- Do not attempt to trim the edges of the liner until you have filled your pond with water.

- Allow a generous margin of liner around the edges of a pond or water feature so you can cover it up with soil or decorative edging.

- Weight down the edges of the liner with bricks or edging stones to hold it in position while you fill the pond with water and smooth out creases.

Blue slate edging stones

MAKING A SUNKEN POND

You can use a flexible liner to create a natural-looking pond in next to no time. Before you begin, calculate how much liner you will need to line the pond (see p. 29). Avoid having to join two pieces of liner to cover the area, as the water is bound to gradually seep out.

USING A FLEXIBLE LINER

2

1 Using your plan as a guide, mark out the shape of the pond on the ground, using a garden hose or rope. If necessary, use canes to hold the hose in position. Unfold the liner and lay it in the sun, as the heat increases its flexibility.

2 Dig out the hole to a depth of 9 in (22 cm) and mark out marginal shelves to a minimum width of 9 in (22 cm). Excavate to the final depth. Use a carpenter's level to check that the top edge of the hole remains level. Remove any sharp stones or roots.

3 Line the hole with a 1–2 in (2.5–5 cm) layer of damp sand and use it to smooth any rough areas. Cover this with a layer of underlay (see p. 23). Loosely drape the liner across the hole. Make sure it is centered, with an even overlap all the way around. Let it sag gently into the hole, then weight the edges with stones.

4 Start filling the pond slowly from a hose. As the pond fills, remove some of the weights to allow the liner to settle snugly into the hole and smooth out any creases – but don't worry unduly about these, as they will not show once the pond is established. Turn off the hose when the water reaches to within 2 in (5 cm) of the rim. Trim any surplus liner using scissors, leaving about 6 in (15 cm) all the way around to allow for settle. Peg or weight this down temporarily.

2

5 Conceal the plastic edge with pavers or stones set in mortar (three parts sand to one part cement), leaving a slight overhang of 1–2 in (2.5–5 cm). Make sure all the plastic is covered. Take great care not to let any mortar fall into the water. If this happens, the pond will have to be emptied and refilled. Wait a few days before adding plants to your new pond. Fish can be introduced after about six weeks.

USING A RIGID LINER

Building a pond using a rigid preformed or molded liner is relatively hassle-free. Problems will only really occur if the liner is installed on the slant. Water full to the brim on one side of the pond, the liner well exposed on the other will be a permanent reminder if you don't get the levels correct right from the start. So make sure you are armed with a carpenter's level and a straight-edged board and check regularly across the width and length of the hole as you go along.

RAISED AND SEMIRAISED PONDS

Rigid, preformed pool units are generally designed to be sunk into the ground. Provided the sides are given strong support, however, they can also be used to construct attractive raised or semiraised pools.

One of the principal disadvantages of a pond installed at ground level is that it will freeze during the winter. This problem can, however, be reduced if the unit is partially buried so that its deep zones are insulated by the surrounding earth. The rigid mold can be concealed with an outer wall of bricks or log-roll edging topped with rocks or coping stones. Alternatively, for a more natural look, fill a gap of about 6 in (15 cm) between wall and liner with topsoil and stock with spreading plants.

SPECIAL FEATURES

Flexible sheet liners are not the only solution to constructing a trickling watercourse or cascade in your water garden. Most water garden specialists now stock a wide range of rigid preformed molds that are quick and easy to install. These include rock pools, tiered waterfalls, and streams. Individual pieces can be overlapped to create cascades of any length to link pools of different levels.

■ **Natural look** Unlike pond liners, which are designed to be submerged, many of the molded watercourses and cascades are produced in natural-looking finishes of rock or stone, which have been specially designed to encourage the growth of algae and lichens. Creatively displayed in a natural setting of rocks and boulders these soon blend in with the rest of the feature.

MOLDED WATERFALL DISPLAY

RAISED POND
A rigid liner can be used to make an attractive raised pond for a patio. Place containers of plants on the edge to conceal any bare areas of liner.

USING A RIGID LINER TO MAKE A SUNKEN POND

- Prop up the liner in position and mark out its shape on the ground using garden hose or rope. Allow an extra 12 in (30 cm) all the way around.
- On a long stick, mark the depth of the pond plus an extra 2 in (5 cm) to allow for bedding sand; also mark the height of any marginal shelves. Use the stick as a guide when digging.
- At every stage of construction, make sure that the liner is level by using a carpenter's level and plank to check along the width and length.
- Cover base with 2 in (2.5 cm) sand.
- Prior to backfilling, ensure that the rim is about 1 in (2.5 cm) below the surrounding ground.
- Once liner is level, wedge it firmly in place with battens.
- Using a hose, start to fill the pond with water. When the level reaches 4–6 in (10–15 cm), remove the battens and start backfilling with sieved soil. Pack spaces beneath shelves. Continue backfilling as the pond level rises until liner and hole are full.
- Run any wiring to the pond before laying the edging so it will be hidden.

RAISED PONDS

An elevated pond will have a greater impact in a smaller garden or patio, where it will provide a strong focal point, particularly if combined with a small fountain. Bear in mind, however, that in areas with cold winters a fully raised pond will freeze solid. This problem can be overcome by sinking part of the pond below ground level. Raised ponds can be constructed using either a flexible sheet liner or a rigid preformed mold.

2

HOW HIGH?

The walls of a raised pond should ideally be the equivalent of about seven courses of brick or stonework high – about 24–28 in (60–70 cm). If this is too tall for your garden design, you can get away with just three or four courses – 18 in (45 cm). This would be a minimum if you want to keep fish, although one obvious solution is to dig out more depth below ground level.

■ **Patio suggestion** On a patio, you could dig down 6–12 in (15–30 cm) and then build the walls 18 in (45 cm) high and top them with wide coping stones. This will give enough depth for fish and waterlilies and a comfortable height for sitting on the wall to feed the fish, take care of the plants, or just to admire the view.

BUILDING THE WALL

Whatever materials you choose for the walls of your pond, they need to be strong enough to hold the weight of the water and to insulate it from summer heat and winter cold.

■ **Construction** A single wall of stone or brick (or wood) will be sufficient to hold a liner, but for better insulation it's preferable to build a double "cavity wall." The inner wall can be made with cheaper concrete blocks or common bricks, reserving the more expensive blocks or bricks for the outer wall. The width of the coping will dictate how far the walls need to be spaced apart. Take into account that the coping should overhang the external wall by ½ in (13 mm) and by a good 1½ in (4 cm) over the water's edge.

MAKING CURVED EDGES

When paving around the top of a circular pond, to avoid the labor and expense of hand-cut "keyed" slabs, buy preformed pavers that are produced specially for this purpose. Most landscape garden centers will stock a good range. Some pavers, such as the ones shown here, can be used as insets in conjunction with normal pavers and will help you turn corners gradually.

CORNER INSET

■ **Foundation** The walls need a good foundation or they will be likely to become unstable. Bed the bottom course on 4–6 in (10–15 cm) of mortar.

WELL LINED

It is important to plan the shape of your raised pond to suit its position in your garden, the materials you intend to use in its construction, and to your competence as a builder. Remember that a circular raised pond is easier to construct than a rectangular one. A raised pond can be lined with a standard flexible sheet liner, or it can be designed around a rigid preformed liner.

SOMEWHERE TO SIT
A flagstone shelf around this regular-shaped pond provides an additional area for ornaments or container plants as well as garden seating.

■ **Preformed rigid liner** A wide range of preformed liners (see pp. 24–25) is available.

■ **Flexible sheet liner** Be warned! A flexible liner in a circular pond will crease horribly, while in a straight-edged construction it will need careful folding at the corners. Buy a good-quality butyl liner: not only will it have to support a lot of weight, a thin liner has few insulating properties. If the pond has a surface area over 40 sq ft (3.7 sq m), you may want to pack insulating material in the cavity between the walls.

■ **Cement** If the walls are made from bricks or blocks bedded on strong foundations on a concrete surround, you may consider rendering the inside with cement. This will then need at least two coats of proprietary pond sealant.

Around the Edge

The edging you choose for your pond is largely a matter of personal taste but it should be compatible with the overall style of your garden and must also hide the liner. Hard edgings often suit a more formal style pond and may include bricks, cobbles, pavers, or even timber. If using these around a sunken pond, in the interests of safety, choose a material that will not become slippery when wet. The natural effect of an informal sunken pond can be greatly increased by growing a range of plants to overhang the edge and provide shade for wildlife.

2

Edging ideas

The appeal of a pond can be greatly enhanced by its surrounding features. Here are a few ideas.

- **Lawn** If setting a pond into an area of lawn make sure the edging sits slightly lower than the grass to make mowing easier.

- **Stepped edge** Try edging a sunken pond in a patio with paving slabs or flagstones to create a gently stepped edge. For maximum effect, choose edging that either matches or contrasts with the patio paving.

- **Hedging** Disguise the rim of a raised pond with a closely clipped hedge, such as dwarf lavender.

- **Steppingstones** These are a popular addition to informal ponds.

Wooden bridge

- **Bridges** A bridge can be used to link one side of a pond with another. You may want to make your own from wooden planks, steel, or iron, or take a look at the range of ready-made bridges at a good aquatic center.

- **Marginal plants** Tall marginal plants, like irises and rushes, will hide the raw edges of a flexible liner.

Preformed paver

Timber ring

Paving slab

■ **Boggy extension** An alternative edging to an informal sunken pond is to create an adjoining bog garden (see pp. 76–77). If possible, this should be built at the same time as the pond, using one large sheet of liner for both features, extended about 3 ft (1 m) out from the edge.

■ **Wildlife access** Allow one or two edging stones to dip into the water.

■ **Paving ideas** Leave gaps between paving around an informal pond, and fill these with cushion-forming plants, such as saxifrage and thyme, or create a surface with small pebbles or cobblestones bedded into cement.

NATURAL EFFECT
Rocks and gravel complement the rich greens of this display of moisture-loving plants to lend a truly natural feel to this pond.

AQUATIC PLANTS

Water plants not only look attractive, they are vital for the overall health of the pond. Without submerged weeds to help to oxygenate the water and floating plants to provide surface shelter from the sun, the water will quickly become foul. When deciding on which plants to choose for your area's climate, select from the range stocked by a local water garden specialist. The five groups of water plants are: waterlilies, oxygenators, deep-water aquatics, marginals, and floaters.

2

WATERLILIES

Although we are most attracted by the blooms of the waterlily, it is the leaves that provide vital shade for fish and prevent algal growth.

■ Place newly planted baskets on brick stacks at a depth of 3–6 in (7.5–15 cm). As the plant produces new leaves and roots, remove the bricks to lower the plant to its recommended depth, which will vary depending on variety and vigor.

■ Waterlilies thrive best in still water. If you run a fountain, make sure the spray falls well away from them.

■ **Planting ratio** One lily to every 25 sq ft (2.3 sq m) of water area. This varies according to size and vigor.

OXYGENATOR PLANT

OXYGENATORS

The health of a pond depends heavily on oxygenating plants. They supply vital oxygen to water and fish, starve out green algae, and break down waste matter produced by fish.

■ Fish use oxygenators as a source of food and as a spawning area.

■ Most aquatic suppliers sell oxygenators as bunches of unrooted cuttings. To plant, either tie a stone to the bottom of each bunch and let it sink into position, or plant in a container of aquatic soil. Plant in the sunniest part of the pond three weeks before introducing any fish.

■ From time to time, trim back excessive growth using a sharp knife, to keep plants bushy and compact.

■ **Planting ratio** One bunch to every 3 sq ft (1 sq m) of water surface.

DEEP-WATER AQUATICS

Generally planted on the bottom of the pond, some deep-water aquatics produce floating leaves and flowers, while others thrust their leaves and flowers above the surface. They help provide shade.

■ **Planting ratio** One plant to every 15 sq ft (1.4 sq m) of water surface.

MARGINALS

Although they provide some shade, marginals are purely decorative plants for the shallow edges of an informal or wildlife pond.

■ Plant in baskets or directly into soil on the pond shelf at the recommended planting depth, measured from the top of the soil to the water level. The planting depth varies from water level to about 6 in (15 cm) below.

■ To acclimatize a new plant, stand the container on bricks and gradually remove these until it is established at the recommended depth.

■ **Planting ratio** One plant to every 5 sq ft (0.5 sq m) of water surface.

FLOATING PLANTS

This group of plants will provide shade in the early days of a pond, before waterlilies are established. They will, however, perish if the temperature drops below freezing.

■ As floating plants take the nutrients they need directly from the water, they can exist without soil. To plant, simply place them on the water's surface.

■ **Planting ratio** One plant to every 10 sq ft (1 sq m) of water surface.

MARGINAL DISPLAY
With its dark, glossy leaves and large, fragrant, white flowers, the arum lily *(Zantedeschia)* is an ideal choice for a more formal setting.

PLANTING UP

Most aquatics are sun-loving plants. While a few plants will grow in the water without soil, the majority must have a suitable soil mix. A medium to heavy loam is best, and specially formulated bags of aquatic soil are available. Never use peat, manure, or fertilizer, as this could pollute the water and encourage the growth of algae.

GENERAL TIPS FOR PLANTING AQUATICS

Aquatics can be planted in special deep-water beds, directly into soil on the bottom of the pond, on marginal shelves, or in specially designed plastic baskets and pots.

■ **Soil depth** The soil on the bottom of the pond must be at least 6 in (15 cm) deep. Cover it with a 1-in (2–3-cm) layer of sand, shingle, or gravel to protect it from fish.

■ **Planting depths** These vary from more than 3 ft (1 m) for some of the strongest-growing waterlilies to just 3 in (7.5 cm) for many marginals.

■ **When to plant** The best time for outdoor plantings is between mid-spring and midsummer. After planting, wait six weeks before introducing fish, water snails, and other wildlife, to allow the water to clear and the plants to settle down.

■ **Plant food** Special aquatic and waterlily foods are available from water garden specialists. These are high in phosphates but low in nitrogen – which would trigger a proliferation of algae and green water. Use according to the manufacturer's instructions.

PLANTING A WATERLILY

1 Line a basket and almost fill with a damp aquatic soil mix. Position the rhizome within 1½ in (4 cm) of the rim. Add soil to ½ in (13 mm) of the rim.

2 Firm the soil, taking care not to damage new shoots. Trim excess liner and cover soil mix with gravel to keep soil in place and protect the roots.

PLANTING BASKETS

Plastic aquatic planting baskets come in a wide range of shapes and sizes to accommodate all kinds of aquatics and make planting up a pond much simpler. The plants will also be easier to look after, as being grown in containers will control their spread. Planting baskets also make life easier when it comes to lifting the plants out when you need to divide and propagate them.

The meshed sides of the containers need to be lined. Special liners are available which keep soil in but allow roots to penetrate. Hessian, which will eventually rot away, can also be used.

Fill containers to within ½ in (13 mm) of the top with soil mix, and finish off with a layer of washed gravel or shingle.

PLANTING BASKETS

STOCKING A NEW POND

When planting your pond, there is a set order you must follow to achieve a healthy balance. Follow the advice and planting ratios given on see pp. 40–41.

- To avoid introducing rogue pests, such as snails or duckweed, or diseases into your pond, check all new plants for signs of any ailments (see pp. 89–90). Always remove new plants from their containers and wash them in cold, running water. Repot each plant in fresh soil mix before standing it in your pond.

- Start by planting oxygenators. Push two or three bunches into soil-filled aquatic baskets and place them at intervals of 2 ft (60 cm) along the bottom of the pond.

- As the water warms up, add a waterlily or two – make sure you choose a variety of the right size and vigor for your pond (see pp. 94–97).

- At the same time, drop in some floating plants to provide shade until the waterlilies establish themselves. In time, it may be necessary to remove some of these floaters as the waterlily pads take over. Plant up marginals, directly into soil or in aquatic baskets, and introduce deep-water aquatics.

- Now be patient. The plants need time to establish, and the water needs time to clear. You will need to wait at least six weeks before introducing fish (see pp. 68–73) – just add a few at a time and allow them to settle.

PROPAGATION

Most water plants can be increased by dividing the rhizome into smaller pieces and planting. Division is best carried out in late spring, every four or five years to prevent overcrowding.

2

SPLITTING A WATERLILY

Too much leafy growth in the center of a waterlily and smaller and fewer flowers are sure signs that the plant needs splitting. Most waterlilies need splitting every three or four years, although some of the smaller hybrids can go six or seven years without attention.

The best time to split a waterlily is late spring or early summer.

- Lift the plant from the water and carefully wash off any soil mix from the rhizome. Remove all opened leaves.

- The waterlily rhizome consists of a main rhizome with a number of sideshoots. Each sideshoot will produce a single healthy plant.

- Using a sharp, clean knife, remove the best sideshoots with a portion of the rhizome. Trim off any long, coarse roots and plant them (see p. 42) individually into pond containers filled with a heavy loam.

- Reposition the new waterlily plants in the pond on bricks at a depth of 2–3 in (5–7.5 cm) of water. As the plant becomes established, you will be able to remove the bricks until the plant is sitting at its final, recommended planting depth.

- Throw away the old central portion of the plant.

TAKING CUTTINGS

1 In spring, use a sharp knife to take a 2–4-in (5–10-cm) cutting just above a pair of leaves. Remove lower leaves and sideshoots.

2 Fill a pot with potting soil mix and insert the cutting. Water well and cover the pot with a plastic bag. Repot once the roots are established.

DIVIDING MARGINALS

Most moisture-loving marginals require little attention and can be simply divided into smaller plants when they've grown too big. Treat marginals as you would any perennial plant.

1 Carefully lift the plant to be divided from the pond and remove it from its container. Wash off any soil. Smaller plants can be gently teased apart by hand, larger specimens may need to be separated using the tines of two garden forks back to back.

2 Pot the offsets up separately. Put some crocks in the bottom of an ordinary 6-in (15-cm) plastic pot and cover these with some aquatic or loam-based soil mix. Place one new plant into each pot and add more soil mix. Firm the soil mix and finish off with a layer of shingle or washed gravel.

3 Don't return the new plants to the pond immediately, as they may float free before new anchoring roots have formed. Place all the pots in a shallow tray and fill this with water. Leave the tray to overwinter in a frost-free environment, such as a greenhouse or cold frame, until the plants are ready to be repotted early the following year. Water them regularly to ensure the soil does not dry out.

4 In late spring or early summer, when strong new shoots are starting to appear and the roots are completely filling the pots, transfer the plants into suitably sized containers filled with loam and return them to the pond.

Gently separate the roots apart with your hands

Once separated, each individual plant can be planted up separately

MOVING WATER

There is nothing quite so relaxing on a hot summer's day as the refreshing sound of a softly babbling stream, the gentle splashing of an ornamental fountain, or the constant rush of water cascading over a rocky slope. As well as soothing our senses, moving water is also of great benefit to fish and plant life as it increases the oxygen content of the water. Even the smallest garden can accommodate a moving water feature. Using one of the many self-assembly kits that are now available from garden centers, installation couldn't be simpler.

FOUNTAIN TIPS

A carefully positioned fountain will greatly influence the style of your water garden. Fountains come in a wide range of sizes and shapes, so before buying one, take a moment to consider the following three points:

- A fountain can empty a pond if the water falls beyond the edge, so make sure the model you choose is not wider than the pond.
- Choose a fountain with a height adjuster so you can regulate the height of the spray. On windy days you may need to turn the fountain off completely to prevent losing too much water.
- If you choose a spray fountain, the fountainhead should be raised just above the surface of the water. You may need to use fountain stem extensions in a deep pond.

ORNAMENTAL TIERED FOUNTAIN

Waterfall or cascade?

For maximum effect, a waterfall needs height, whereas a cascade can work well with a drop of just 6 in (15 cm).

■ Preformed fiberglass stone-effect liners (see p. 34) are available for making waterfalls and streams, but can restrict the length, width, and color of your design. The overall shape of the feature will still need softening with plants and real stones.

CASCADES OF WATER
In a small garden, a cascade of three or more shallow drops looks more natural than one high waterfall.

■ Heavy-duty flexible sheet liner will enable you to to design and construct a more natural-looking waterfall or stream. Separate sheets will be needed for each tier; always overlap higher sheets over the top of lower ones. Make the feature look more natural by placing stones and plants at the sides and bottom.

PUMPS AND FILTERS

Fountains, waterfalls, cascades, and filters all require an electric pump to move water through them. Pumps are available in all shapes and sizes, to suit every kind of water feature. Small submersible pumps operate at low voltage from a transformer and are safe and easy to install. Large features need surface pumps powered by the main electrical supply and should be installed by a qualified electrician.

2

PUMPS

Before buying a pump, work out what you want it to do and discuss your requirements with an expert. The two categories of pump are:

■ **Feature pumps** These are designed to move water through features such as fountains and waterfalls and may be submersible or above the surface. Most submersible feature pumps also have an integral filter.

■ **Filter pumps** These are designed to deliver water through a filter. They are capable of filtering out small solids in the water.

INSTALLING A PUMP

- Position the pump on a level surface, such as bricks or a special mounting platform, just clear of the bottom of the pond. This prevents debris from being sucked into the pump and clogging the works.
- Connect the pump to the electricity supply via a weatherproof cable connector to the extension lead. Conceal this beneath paving.
- Disconnect both the pump and the filter and remove them from the water during winter.

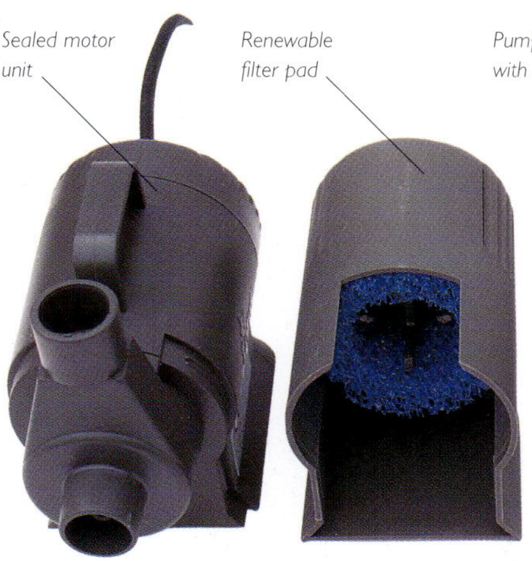

ELECTRICAL POND PUMP WITH BUILT-IN FILTER SYSTEM

SOLIDS-HANDLING PUMP TO WORK WITH A SEPARATE FILTER

2

FILTERS

In a well-stocked, established garden pond, the plants should keep the water clean and create a healthy environment for fish. In a new pond, however, this may take time, during which the water will go green and murky, due to the growth of algae. If this is the case, you may want to consider installing a filter system or ultraviolet purifier, which helps fight against the growth of green algae. Pond filters, most of which are sited outside the pond, generally combine the following methods of filtration:

- **Mechanical filters** Solid particles are strained out from the water as it flows through the filter.

- **Biological filters** The water flows through several layers of mineral materials, which have a large surface area on which bacteria flourish. These bacteria break down and purify waste products and gases on which green algae thrive.

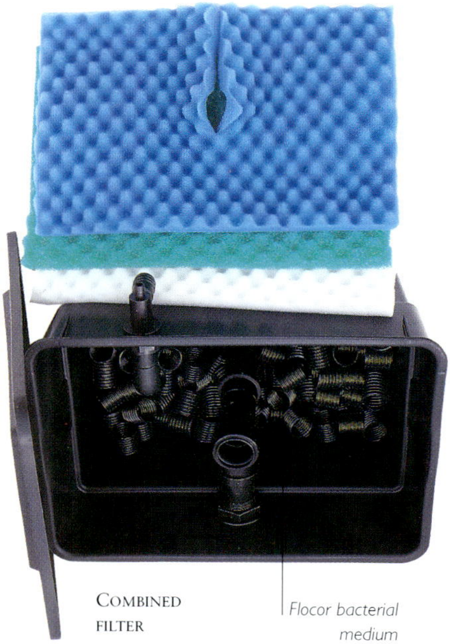

COMBINED FILTER

Flocor bacterial medium

Water garden specialists offer a wide selection of filters. To be sure you select the right filter for your pond, ask the advice of an expert. If you have a very small pond, a simple algicide may be a cheaper solution.

SPRAY EFFECTS USING A SUBMERSIBLE PUMP

The spray pattern of a fountain is dictated by the size and placing of holes in the nozzle and by the height and width of the water, which are dictated by the flow adjuster controls.

Use a small submersible pump for spray heights of up to 4 ft (1.2 m); a larger submersible pump up to 7 ft (2.2 m), and a high-head exterior pump for heights exceeding 7 ft (2.2. m).

SURFACE JET

WHIRLING SPRAY

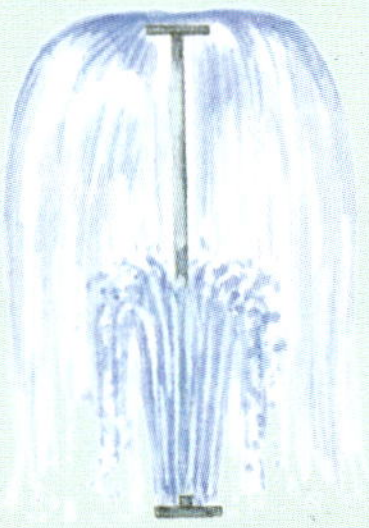

TIFFANY JET

GEYSER FOUNTAIN

Lighting

Any water feature can be enhanced by the creative use of garden lighting. There is a wide range of spotlights and and wide-beam lights available, some of which can be floated or submerged to illuminate the water. These can create a really dramatic spectacle at night, when the water magnifies their effect.

2

Surface lighting effects

The secret of good lighting is to highlight certain areas or features, leaving other parts in darkness. Floodlights produce a diffuse pool of light covering a wide area, while the beam of a spotlight will light up a specific plant or feature.

For around the pond, you can find both surface-mounted lights and spiked models that can be set in a border or lawn. Globe and searchlight styles will give general illumination; mushroom and tiered lights are used for downlighting.

Low-voltage spotlight

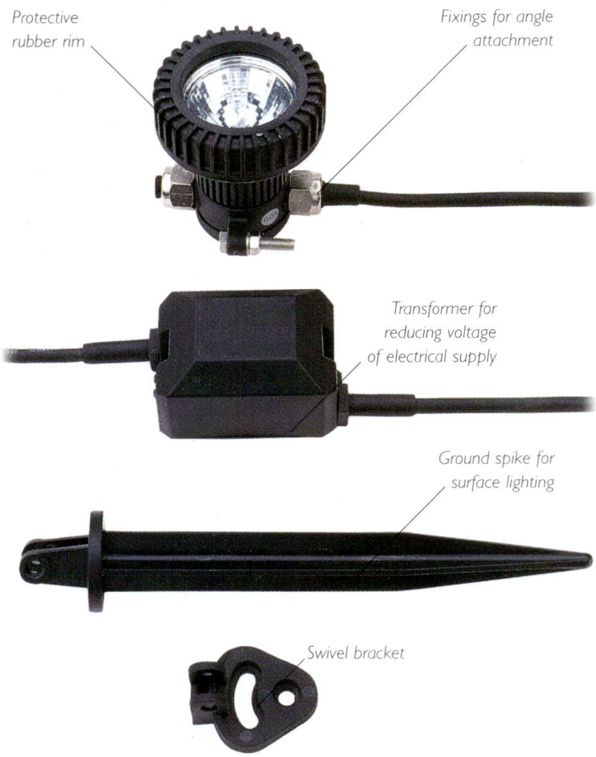

Quick Fix

- Low-voltage lights operate by means of a reduced-voltage supply via a transformer, so installation is safe and straightforward.
- If possible, run the cable under edging stones around the pond where there is no risk of someone accidentally cutting through it while gardening.
- If you have to bury cable, it must be covered with a protective steel sleeve.
- Solar-powered lights do not require any cables – just a battery to be charged via a transformer.

SUBMERSIBLE GLOBE LIGHT

MINI-HIGHLIGHTER

2

SUBMERGED LIGHTING

Underwater lights cast a magical spell over a water feature after dark. Floating, submerged, or clustered around a fountain, they produce an impressive effect, particularly when various colored filters are utilized.

■ **Purchasing tips** Check before you buy whether the lights are for surface or underwater use. The flex of submerged lights will need to be weighted down using a smooth stone. Do not place the lights deeper than 1 in (2.5 cm) below the surface, otherwise the effect will be lost.

■ **Maintenance** Regularly hose off any debris that collects on the lights. From time to time, you will also need to remove the lights from the water, wash them in warm soapy water, then rinse them and put them back.

■ **Caution** Remember to disconnect the power before handling lights or when taking them out of the water.

LIGHT SHOW
A submersible light positioned below a gushing fountain creates a magical illusion after dark. Different moods and effects can be achieved by the creative use of colored bulbs and lenses.

ORNAMENTS

Although plants and fish are ornamentation enough for most ponds, during the colder months, when the plants have died down and the fish are inactive, it is pleasant to have something decorative to look at, particularly in the case of a formal pond in a prominent position or themed garden design.

2

ORNAMENT IDEAS

A wide range of ornaments and figures are available to add extra interest to your pond.

■ **Small features** Most garden centers stock a wide range of stone figures most of which are discreet enough to blend harmoniously by the side of even the smallest informal pond.

■ **Focal points** Some ornaments, such as classical statuettes, make ideal focal features positioned either on the edge or in the center of a pond. When planning the planting of the pond, leave clear areas of water around the figure to optimize the effect of the reflection. You could also try laying an old stone urn on its side amid plants or on gravel to add a touch of fantasy.

SHIPWRECKED TREASURE

LEAPING FISH

WELL CONTAINED

■ **Containers** Terra-cotta, glazed, wooden, and even plastic pots and planters will help break up an expanse of hard landscaping around a pond, particularly on a patio, where an attractive display of color can soften the overall formality – just make sure the pots are raised off the ground so water can drain away.

Don't forget that containers can also be planted up to provide a colorful display throughout the year – even during winter and early spring. Miniature conifers, winter-flowering heathers and pansies, early-flowering spring bulbs, and trailing ivy will brighten the darkest day. The scope is endless, and a visit to a local garden center will give you plenty of inspiration – both for pots and plants.

Small water features

SMALL WATER FEATURES

Even the smallest garden can accommodate a water feature. Any watertight container can be pressed into service: an old sink or simply a wooden half-barrel will be deep enough for a miniature waterlily and one or two other aquatics. Even a 12-in (30-cm) terra-cotta pot – with any drainage holes sealed – can be "planted" with an iris or two and a couple of floating aquatics. And you don't need a pond to enjoy a fountain: there are self-contained units that just need filling with water and the power switched on. Cobble ponds and millstone features are a safer way to introduce water to a garden where there are children about, while a simple birdbath will attract a host of feathered visitors to the garden. Find out more about creating a water garden in miniature in this chapter.

POTS OF WATER

It is amazing how soon a container of water standing out on the patio will attract wildlife, from birds dropping in for a quick drink and a bath, to a frog or toad seeking a more permanent residence. No container is too small to grow water plants in, even an old kitchen sink can be used to display a waterlily. And by choosing plants carefully, a wooden half-barrel or a large glazed pot can provide a home for a variety of aquatics.

AQUATICS ON HIGH

Where space is limited, such as on a balcony, a simple water feature can be created in a tub. Mail-order kits containing a tub, plants, baskets, and fertilizer are widely available. Plants for such a feature include a dwarf waterlily (e.g. *Nymphaea* 'Pygmaea Helvola'), blue flag *(Iris versicolor)*, milfoil *(Myriophyllum)*, and water hyacinth *(Eichhornia crassipes)*.

BUBBLING OVER
Almost any container can be adapted to make a stylish water feature. A small fountain can be added to create a gentle bubbling sound.

CLEAN AND WATERTIGHT

- Scrub out your container with clean water and a stiff brush. Do not use detergent or a cleaning agent.
- Seal any drainage holes to make sure the container is watertight.
- Do not use wooden containers that have held wood preservative, oil, or tar, as any residue will pollute the water and form scum on the surface.
- Water in a barrel or pot is not a suitable outdoor environment for keeping fish.

Wooden half-barrels can be bought from most garden centers or architectural salvage specialists. New ones will usually have been made watertight already, but to be sure there are no residues in the wood that could harm plants, it is a good idea to paint the inside with a proprietary sealant. Old barrels will usually require lining with a length of flexible liner (see p. 30).

FULL TO THE BRIM
Two wooden half-barrels arranged at different levels create a compact water feature that brings sound and movement to a small garden.

BARRELS AND SINKS

A miniature pond in a half-barrel or sink will create a focus on a balcony, terrace, or small patio, or add interest to a corner of your garden. They can be freestanding, perhaps surrounded by plants, or sunk into the ground – which gives some protection against frost.

A SIMPLE BARREL GARDEN

Before planting up your barrel, check for leaks. Fill it with water, mark the level, and let it stand for a few days. If the level drops, you will need to re-waterproof it before it can be used. It is also a good idea to plant up the barrel in its intended position as it will be too heavy to move once it is full. Support the barrel on bricks to allow air to circulate underneath.

3

1 Partly fill the barrel with bricks to create a range of planting levels. Check that the depth of the bricks corresponds with the correct planting depths of the plants you have selected.

2 Plant up planting baskets (see p. 42) with your selected plants and position in the barrel. Choose curved baskets that will fit snugly around the edges. Sprinkle baskets with gravel to keep soil mix in place. Add decorative rocks and gently fill with water.

CHOOSING YOUR BARREL

- Choose a barrel about 2 ft (60 cm) in diameter, with a minimum depth of 12 in (30 cm), equivalent to a capacity of about 10 gallons (45.5 liters).
- If you are not going to use the barrel immediately, keep about 2–3 in (5–8 cm) of water in the bottom to stop it from drying out – which could cause cracks to develop in the wood.
- Block drainage holes by hammering in lengths of wooden dowling. There is no need to seal them, as they will expand when wet and fit tight.
- Check that the inside surfaces have been properly sealed and that there are no leaks.

3 Once your barrel is full of water, position the rocks to conceal the edges of the planting baskets and consider adding a small ornament. The planted barrel will look particularly effective perhaps set amid rocks and flowers in a sunny corner. Check the water level regularly and refresh it if you notice that water has evaporated. Thin out the plants if they start to look overcrowded.

SINK GARDENS

If you're lucky enough to come across one, you can transform an old galvanized sink into an easy summer water feature for a cool corner of your garden. Simply clean out the sink thoroughly (see p. 54) and make sure it is entirely watertight. Then fill with water and stock with suitable water plants, such as dwarf waterlilies.

MAKING A TUFA SINK

Transform an old glazed porcelain sink into an original summer water garden by coating its exterior in tufa to create a natural-looking exterior.

- Clean the sink well (see p. 54).
- Make up the hypertufa: 2 parts peat, 1 part sand, and 1 part cement, made into a stiff mix with water.
- Score the sink's exterior with a glass cutter and coat with a bonding agent.
- While this is still sticky, spread on a ½-in (13-mm) layer of hypertufa. Plug the drainhole and cover with sealant.
- Leave the hypertufa to harden – this will take about two weeks.
- Fill the sink with water, and stock with a selection of aquatic plants (see pp. 58–59).

AQUATICS FOR POTS

Water plants grown in small containers will need more attention than those in a pond, as they can quickly outgrow their space and need regular thinning and cutting back. However, by selecting plants of differing heights, textures, and colors, you can create a stunning ensemble that will quickly become an established feature.

PLANTING AND CARE

■ Although a water garden in a container is best planted up in the spring, planting can continue until midsummer.

■ Plants in a wooden half-barrel are best grown in aquatic pots and baskets, rather than in a layer of soil spread on the floor of the barrel. Not only will this extend the barrel's life, but it will also make caring for the plants easier.

3

■ Submerged plants are best planted in 1-pint (0.5-liter) pots while dwarf waterlilies will need at least 3-pint (1.5-liter) pots. Marginal plants can go in small round or square pots. All these pots should be lined first. It may be necessary to stand the pots of marginals on bricks so that they are at their correct planting depth.

■ Use an aquatic planting soil mix or heavy topsoil with a clay content. Firm plants in, then cover the surface with a light dressing of gravel.

■ Aquatic plants in a ceramic or terra-cotta pot can be grown in a 3-in (7.5-cm) layer of soil spread over the bottom. Again, top the soil with a layer of gravel after planting.

■ If using soil from the garden, it must not have been given a recent application of fertilizer. Sieve it first to remove any large stones.

PLANT CATEGORIES

Water plants that suit being grown in containers such as half-barrels or large patio tubs can be divided into three categories:

- **Submerged plants** These are the oxygenating plants and most of their foliage will remain below the water level.
- **Lilies and lilylike plants** These have their root systems on the bottom but their flowers and foliage will be in full view on the surface.
- **Marginal plants** These like their roots in the water but their flowers and foliage are held above the surface.

■ Take care not to disturb the pot's contents when filling it with water.

■ The water level needs to be topped up regularly, as a surprising amount will be lost through evaporation.

■ Remove faded flowers and yellowing leaves as they appear.

■ If winter months are particularly cold, and your water feature is in danger of freezing solid, if possible, move the barrel under cover – in a greenhouse or sunroom. If not, it would be best to drain the water out, and provide a temporary winter home for any plants.

SUBMERGED

Plant these in plastic containers and place them on the bottom of the barrel.

Callitriche hermaphroditica*, syn. *C. autumnalis
Water starwort

Crassula helmsii*, syn. *Tillaea recurva

Eleocharis acicularis
Spike rush, hair grass

Lagarosiphon major*, syn. *Elodea crispa

MARGINALS

Plant marginals in containers and stand them on bricks, if necessary, to allow 2–3 in (5–8 cm) of water above the crown of the plant.

***Acorus gramineus* 'Variegatus'**
Japanese rush

Calla palustris
Bog arum

***Caltha palustris* 'Flore Pleno'**
Double yellow kingcup

Eriophorum angustifolium
Cotton grass

***Houttuynia cordata* 'Plena'**

Iris versicolor Blue flag

***Juncus effusus* 'Spiralis'**
Corkscrew rush

Myosotis palustris
Water forget-me-not

Sagittaria sagittifolia
Arrowhead

Typha minima
Miniature bulrush, reedmace

3

DWARF WATERLILIES (*NYMPHAEA*)

Select miniature varieties of waterlily that require a planting depth of 12 in (30 cm), spread no more than 2 ft (60 cm), and have flowers 2–4 in (5–10 cm) across. Plant only one waterlily to each barrel or tub.

***N.* 'Andreana'** (yellow to red)

N. candida (white)

***N.* 'Caroliniana Nivea'** (white)

***N.* 'Firecrest'** (pink)

***N.* 'Froebelii'** (red)

***N.* 'Graziella'** (red)

***N.* 'Laydekeri Lilacea'** (pink)

***N.* 'Laydekeri Purpurata'** (red)

***N.* 'Pygmaea Alba'** (white)

***N.* 'Pygmaea Helvola'** (yellow)

***N.* 'Pygmaea Rubra'** (pink)

N. 'CAROLINIANA NIVEA'

LILYLIKE

Plant these in plastic containers and place them on the bottom of the barrel. In time, the foliage and flowers will rise to the surface.

Aponogeton distachyos
Water hawthorn, Cape pondweed

Hydrocharis morsus-ranae
Frogbit

Nuphar minima
Yellow pond lily

Nymphoides peltata*, syns. *Villarsia bennettii*, *Limnanthemum nymphoides
Fringed water lily, water fringe, yellow floating heart

SPOUTS AND BUBBLES

The sound and sight of water, splashing and sparkling in the sunlight as it spurts from a miniature fountain or bubble feature can alter the mood of your garden, creating an atmosphere of calm. All you need to create such a feature are a pump, access to a power supply, a modest reservoir of water, and an outlet through which the water will flow.

SPOUTING WATER

A basic low-voltage electric pump can be used to recirculate water from a modest reservoir through a wide range of decorative waterspouts and fountains to create a variety of magical features that will introduce sound and movement into your garden. Make a visit to your local water garden specialist to look at the wide range of features offered.

3

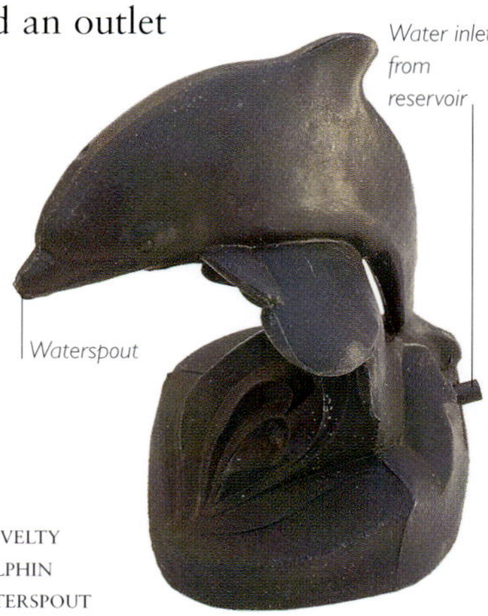

NOVELTY DOLPHIN WATERSPOUT

WATER TROUGH

Many come in kit form and can be assembled using basic tools and a minimum of expertise. Most will be up and running within a few hours of purchase and can be sited anywhere in the garden – even in the shadiest corner.

- **Novelty** Most garden centers stock a wide range of small items, such as the dolphin waterspout above, through which water can be pumped to create a novelty feature.

- **Fountain and trough** An integral upright outlet coupled with a stone trough makes a useful alternative to a wall fountain in a garden where there are no strong walls to support the outlet. This feature would look perfect surrounded by lush foliage plants against a trellis or even across a corner to conceal a leggy hedge.

WALL FOUNTAINS

To create a striking wall fountain, all you need is a wall strong enough to bear the weight of the fountain and an electrical outlet to power the pump. Wall fountain outlet plaques are available in real and artificial stone, cast iron, tile, concrete, terra cotta, copper, and even convincingly textured plastic and fiberglass.

A popular choice for a very small garden is a classical-style mask, where water spilling from the mouth collects in a reservoir below. This can be a stone bowl, or even an old sink disguised by plants. The pump may be submerged in the pool or in a concealed chamber nearby.

Make sure the flow of water from the mouth is strong enough to spout into the center of the reservoir pool without splashing over the sides, otherwise you will find that you constantly need to top it up.

GURGLING GARGOYLES
Create an atmospheric, grotto-like feel on a shady wall by surrounding the mask with ivy – both green and variegated – ferns, and mosses.

Bubble features

Gurgling millstone fountains and pebble pools are an excellent way of introducing a water feature into a garden where there are children about or where a conventional pond is not practical. Both are easy to install, need little maintenance, and suit a patio, gravel bed, or border.

These features can be sited in a shady spot but will need access to an earthed electricity supply to power the pump. Turn to pages 17 and 48 for tips on installing pumps and electrical equipment. If in any doubt, always consult a qualified electrician.

No external water supply is needed for these features, as the same water is recirculated from an integral reservoir. In winter, they should be disconnected, drained, and the pump removed and stored indoors.

3

Miniature lotus flower bubble feature

Millstone fountains

Original millstones are becoming increasingly difficult to find, in addition to which they are very heavy to move; however, it is now possible to buy fiberglass replicas, often as part of a self-assembly kit.

The pump is placed in a reservoir directly beneath the millstone from which a delivery pipe leads up through the hole at the center.

If a millstone is too big for your garden, smaller features are available, such as the lotus flower shown above, which work on the same principle.

BUBBLING MILLSTONE
A millstone with water rippling gently over its surface makes an attractive and restful feature in a setting of differently sized pebbles and rocks.

PEBBLE SPOUT

3

MAKING A PEBBLE POOL

A pebble pool not only looks natural, it is a safe and trouble-free way of bringing moving water into a garden and can be installed at ground level or in a raised bed. Kits ranging in diameter from 2 ft (60 cm) to 6 ft (1.8 m) are readily available. A kit usually comprises a water reservoir, a lid to keep leaves and debris out, a lining, pump, fountain, and cabling.

■ Dig out a hole to take the water reservoir – about 10–12 in (25–30 cm) deep should suffice.

■ Run electricity to the feature to power the pump.

■ Fill the reservoir with water and install the pump and fountainhead.

■ Put the lid over the water reservoir.

■ Arrange the pebbles, and switch on the fountain.

■ The pump will circulate the water over the pebbles and back into the reservoir again.

ROCKS AND BOULDERS

BLUE SLATE

Some pebble-pool kits include the decorative pebbles; however, if not, a whole range of pebbles and cobbles in different sizes and colors is available at most larger garden centers. You can of course make your own feature using drilled boulders or rocks, or just a jet of water falling onto cobbles.

DRILLED BOULDERS

MINI-TIRE FEATURE

With a bit of imagination, you can make a water feature out of almost anything. This novelty feature is made with a premolded plastic reservoir and lid, a low-voltage submersible pump, a ceramic fountain feature, an old car tire, river rocks, and plants in containers.

MAKING UP THE KIT

1 Plan where you want to position your water feature in the garden. Once it is planted up and filled with water it will be too heavy and awkward to move. You will need to choose a site close to a supply of electricity to power the pump. Make sure the dimensions of the plastic reservoir in the kit fit inside the tire.

ALTERNATIVE IDEAS

Instead of placing the reservoir inside a tire, you could try burying it in the ground and surrounding it with plants. Instead of rocks, experiment with differently colored gravel. Alternatively, you could partially sink the reservoir and heap earth around it, which could then be planted up.

3

2 Line the ground at the base of the tire with a layer of fine sand. Lower the plastic reservoir so its upper rim fits snugly over the top of the tire.

3 Position the pump on the base of the reservoir. If the pump does not have its own built-in feet, place it on top of a few stones to ensure that water can flow underneath. Feed the electrical cable from the pump through the molded feed channel and fill the reservoir with water. Place the cover on the reservoir so the delivery pipe from the pump protrudes through the central hole.

4 Place the ceramic ammonite shell feature over the pump spout and decorate the cover of the reservoir with a layer of pebbles and rocks.

3

5 Complete the effect of your water feature by surrounding it with decorative plants. These can be planted directly into the soil or, as here, in containers to continue the shell theme. Switch on the pump and enjoy!

BIRDBATHS

Perhaps the smallest and simplest water feature, a birdbath positioned within sight of the house can bring you hours of pleasure watching the visitors splashing in the water. Choose from a wide range of styles and materials to blend in with your garden.

3

SIZE AND STYLES

Birdbaths are available in a variety of designs and styles. They can be mounted on a pedestal, supported on a post, hung from a chain, or sunk into the ground.

■ **Homemade bath** Sink a trash-can lid, flowerpot base, or large dish into the soil. It should have sloping sides that allow small birds to bathe at the edges and must have a central depth of about 3½ in (9 cm) to accommodate larger birds.

■ **Position** Birds will not use a birdbath unless they feel safe, so site the bath close to cover where they can take refuge to dry and preen.

■ **Check the water** In hot weather, keep the water level topped up. In winter, if the water surface freezes, melt the ice. In prolonged periods of frost, a rubber ball floating on the surface will provide access to the water. Never use antifreeze or salt, which are harmful to wildlife.

■ **Cleaning** Periodically clean out the birdbath with clean water and a scrub brush. Do not use chemicals or detergent.

CLASSICAL PEDESTAL BIRDBATH

DECORATIVE METAL BIRDBATH

Stake is driven into the ground to support the birdbath

Life in the pond

4

LIFE IN THE POND

One of the charms of a water garden is that it will quickly start to teem with plant and animal life – whether it is the ornamental fish that you introduce, the frogs, toads, and newts that take up residence, or the insects, and birds that soon become frequent visitors.

In this chapter, we look at choosing, buying, and caring for ornamental fish and ways of encouraging frogs and other amphibians to a bog garden or wildlife pond.

However, unwelcome guests, such as herons and birds of prey, may also take an interest in your pond, and the chapter looks at humane methods of dissuading them.

4

ORNAMENTAL FISH

Fish bring life and interest to any pond, and there is nothing quite so restful as watching them as they glide effortlessly between strands of pondweed and lily stems. Today a wide range of exotic ornamental species is available in a variety of sizes and colors; however, the basic requirements of all healthy fish remain the same – clean, well-aerated water and adequate space, shade, and food.

BASIC REQUIREMENTS

Most ornamental, cold-water fish are resilient and need little attention: just clean water, plenty of oxygen, some shade, and room to swim and grow. Koi carp require at least a 3-ft (1-m) depth of water, while smaller fish, such as goldfish and shubunkin can survive in just 18 in (45 cm). Before buying fish, think about how visible they will be in your pond. White, yellow, orange, and red goldfish and the more active golden orfe are a safe choice as their colors contrast with the dark water and they tend to stay close to the surface.

INTRODUCING THE FISH

The best time to introduce fish to a pond is late spring to summer, when the water temperature reaches at least 50°F (10°C). Wait at least six weeks after planting before stocking a new pond with fish. This will give the plants time to root and allow the pond to find its correct balance. The level of stocking varies according to planting levels, filtration, volume of water, surface area, water movement, aeration, and the level to which you intend to maintain the pond. See the box opposite for a general guide to stocking levels.

BUYING YOUR FISH

Fish can be bought from water garden suppliers, garden centers, and even mail order. Choose fish that appear healthy and active – one diseased fish can affect others already in your pond. Look for an erect dorsal fin (on the fish's back), bright eyes, and smooth scales. Never buy a fish that has white spots the size of a pinhead along its body or one that shows any sign of damage. Select medium-sized fish, about 3–5 in (7–12 cm) in length.

BRINGING THEM HOME

To transport fish home, place them in polyethylene bags, half filled with water and then inflated with air or oxygen and sealed. In the car, place the bags in cardboard boxes and protect the fish from light.

STOCKING LEVELS

If fish are to survive, it is important not to overstock your pond. Use the following ratio to work out the **maximum** number of fish you can introduce into your pond.

- A water surface area of 1 ft x 1 ft (30 cm x 30 cm) will support a fish 2 in (5 cm) long, from nose to tail. This means that a pond of 100 sq ft (9 sq m) would accommodate 200 in (500 cm) of fish. This could work out as 100 2-in (5-cm) fish, 50 4-in (10-cm) fish, or 25 8-in (20-cm) fish, or a mixture of lengths as long as the total length does not exceed the maximum of 200 in (500 cm).
- Koi carp are the exception, as one large fish needs an area of at least 4 ft x 3 ft (120 cm x 90 cm).

ACCLIMATIZING YOUR FISH

FLOATING BAG ON POND SURFACE

GENTLY RELEASING FISH INTO POND

Fish do not like sudden changes in temperature so once you get them home, you will need to spend some time acclimatizing them to their new home.

- Float the sealed bag with the fish inside on the surface of the pond for about half an hour. This allows the water in the bag to reach the same temperature as the water in the pond. If the pond is in full sun, shade the bag with a newspaper.
- Gently open the bag to allow some pond water in. Leave it for about 10 minutes, then carefully slip – do not tip – the fish into the pond. It will probably head straight for the bottom and hide itself away among the foliage until it has become familiar with its new surroundings.

4

FEEDING REQUIREMENTS

In a pond, fish are able to feed on the minute organisms and algae in their surroundings. You will, however, need to give supplementary food in spring and summer when they are most active. Feeding time also provides an opportunity to examine the fish for any signs of damage or disease.

■ **When to feed** Feed the fish once or twice a day, preferably at the same time and in the same place. If you have a fountain, you may find that switching it off brings the fish up to the surface. After five minutes, use a net to remove any uneaten food or this will decay and cause the water to become murky and polluted.

■ **Proprietary foods** There are many proprietary brands of fish food available, either as floating pellets or as fish sticks. Floating foods are preferable to flaked foods, which, if uneaten, will sink to the bottom to decay and pollute the water.

■ **Live foods** To vary the diet, live foods, such as daphnia and shrimp are available. If you are not squeamish, you could also feed them on chopped worms from the compost heap.

■ **Holidays** If you go away for a couple of weeks, the fish should be able to survive quite happily without any supplementary feeding.

HANDLING FISH

Fish are easily damaged by poor handling, so it is important to learn how to use a net for catching and releasing them.

- Single out the fish you want to catch.
- Very gently place the net in the water about 12–15 in (30–38 cm) away from the fish.
- Hold the net still for a minute or two before approaching the fish.
- Sweep the net to the underside of the fish, then lift gently.
- To release a fish from the net, lower the net gently into the water and allow the fish to swim out of the net at its own pace.

CATCHING FISH

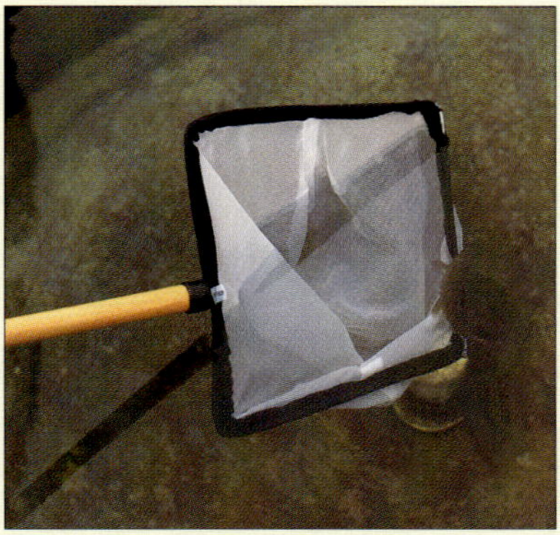

RELEASING FISH

4

WINTER HIBERNATION

In cold weather, fish will stay in the deepest part of the pond, almost in a state of hibernation. However, a mild spell will bring them up to the surface. When the water temperature reaches 50°F (10°C), start to feed them every couple of days with a wheatgerm-rich food. Supplement their diet of floating food with a few chopped-up worms and daphnia.

In more extreme climates, where there is a risk that the pond may freeze solid, you will need to house your fish in a temporary pond in a cool part of the house or in a shed until temperatures rise in spring.

FISH HIDE

Hides offer fish protection from the hot sun

KEEPING FISH HAPPY AND HEALTHY

- Don't overstock the pond (see p. 69).
- Give the fish plenty of natural shade – waterlily leaves and other floating plants will provide this.
- Make sure the fish get plenty of oxygen by maintaining water movement. This is particularly important during a heat wave, and in periods of thundery weather. It may be necessary to keep the fountain or waterfall going all night.
- Take care when using insecticides or weed-killers near the pond to prevent spray drifting over the water.
- Water used to fill the pond should not have been stored in a metal container.
- Where a lawn surrounds a sunken pond, make sure that lawn treatments are not applied close to the pond's edge where they can be washed into the pond by rain.
- Soil used for planting underwater baskets and containers should be free from chemicals and fertilizers.
- To give your fish an extra boost in spring, food and vitamin supplements are available that will gradually release valuable minerals into the water.

FOOD TABLET

VITAMIN BOOSTER

VARIETIES OF FISH

From common goldfish and shubunkin to golden orfe and beautiful, but expensive, koi carp, you can choose from a wide variety of ornamental fish in a rainbow of colors for your garden pond. Here are just a few of the varieties you are likely to come across.

GOLDFISH VARIETIES

■ **Common goldfish** These popular yellow, orange, and red fish are inexpensive to buy and, given the right conditions, they can grow to 15 in (38 cm) and may live for 20 years. They breed easily.

■ **Shubunkin** The scales of a shubunkin produce a mottled, multicolored effect – blue, red, white, yellow, even violet and black. Shubunkins grow up to 15 in (38 cm) long and breed easily.

■ **Comet** With longer fins and tails, comets move faster and more elegantly than common goldfish. The red and white variety is known as the Sarasa Comet. They breed easily.

■ **Fantail** The metallic-orange fantail reaches 3½ in (9 cm) and breeds easily.

SHUBUNKIN
The shubunkin's scales are almost transparent, allowing pigment cells below to show through, producing a mottled multicolored effect.

4

SPECIALTY KOI CARP
Highly bred and exotic, koi carp are judged by their scale types, colors, and patterns – single-color, two-color, and multicolor.

OTHER FISH

■ **Tench** Both green and golden tench are sometimes sold as pond scavengers to remove waste material from the bottom of a pond – which is where they spend their lives. Put one in your pond and you may never see it again. Goldfish do the job just as well and are more visible.

■ **Koi carp** Colorful, active and long-lived, koi can become so tame they will feed from your hand. They are not, however, suitable for the average-sized garden pond as they can grow to more than 3 ft (1 m) in length – and, unlike other fish, they will carry on growing, even in the most cramped conditions. They have a tendency to stir up mud from the bottom and eat soft-leaved aquatics.

■ **Golden orfe** These golden or salmon-orange colored fish move around rapidly, just below the surface of the water, scavenging for insects. They should be easily seen, but these are timid fish when small and will hide among the plants if there are just one or two of them. Introduce six or so, and they will patrol as a shoal.

Golden orfes grow up to 18–20 in (45–50 cm) long and so they need a pond measuring 35 sq ft (3.25 sq m) or more. They also have a high oxygen requirement, so there needs to be some movement of water, such as that provided by a fountain or waterfall.

■ **Golden rudd** Similar in appearance to a golden orfe, but not so visible in the water, the golden rudd is suitable for a smaller pond as it grows no more than 6–9 in (15–23 cm). It also needs less oxygen, but it does like higher water temperatures.

■ **Rosy minnow** The rosy minnow and the three-spined stickleback are both well suited for a true wildlife pond, moving around in shoals, and growing no bigger than 3 in (7 cm). Their dull coloring tends to make them difficult to see.

A WILDLIFE POND

Insects, birds, amphibians, and mammals will always be attracted to a pond, especially if it has been carefully planned to imitate nature. As natural wetland habitats shrink, garden ponds, however small, provide vital sanctuaries and breeding grounds for a wide range of increasingly threatened wildlife. Native plants are more attractive to indigenous wildlife, so try to include as many of these in your plantings as possible.

A POND FOR WILDLIFE

To construct a successful wildlife pond, follow the same steps as for an ornamental pond (see pp. 32–33), with one or two modifications.

■ Keep the shape of the pond very informal and at least 2 ft (60 cm) deep. Create variations in depth to provide different habitats. Deeper water protects wildlife in winter.

IMITATING NATURE
The careful selection of a range of native water plants will create a natural environment to attract birds, insects, and amphibians.

■ Create a gentle slope, perhaps in the form of a pebbly beach, on one side of the pond to give wildlife access to the water.

■ Include an area for growing bog and marginal plants to provide cover.

■ Line the pond with a heavy-duty butyl liner on a bed of sand. Place a further 2-in (5-cm) layer of sand on top of the liner and cover with a 2–3-in (5–7.5-cm) layer of soil (medium to heavy loam or specially formulated aquatic soil).

4

VENUS FLYTRAP
(DIONAEA MUSCIPULA)

PLANTS TO GROW

Try to grow a selection of native plants, which will attract a greater variety of insects and butterflies. For inspiration, look at the kind of plants growing around ponds and streams in the countryside where you live. Do not pick or collect wild plants.

■ **Surface cover** If space allows, grow the common white waterlily *(Nymphaea alba)*. In smaller ponds floating heart *(Nymphoides peltata)* or water hawthorn *(Aponogeton distachyos)* give good surface cover.

■ **Marginals** Plant tall marginals, such as bog bean (*Menyanthes*), bulrushes *(Typha)*, cotton grass *(Eriophorum)*, the water gladioli *(Butomus)*, and the yellow flag *(Iris pseudacorus)*. In warmer climates where there is no danger of frost, a few Venus flytraps *(Dionaea muscipula)* will add interest and attract and even catch insects.

■ **Oxygenators** Choose, among others, *Callitriche stagnalis*.

NO GOLDFISH

Goldfish are not advised for a wildlife pond, doing more harm than good, as they love to eat tadpoles. Although frogs will continue to use the pond to spawn each year, any goldfish will eat all the tadpoles long before they turn into froglets.

If you want to include fish in your wildlife pond, larger sticklebacks can be introduced, although these will also occasionally prey on tadpoles.

TAMING NATURE

Maintaining a balance between nature and garden requires some vigilance.

• Control the spread of plants such as reeds and flag irises or they will start to monopolize marginal plantings.

• In summer, skim blanketweed and other algal growth from the surface. After removing it from the water, leave it on the pondside for a while to allow any amphibians to escape.

4

A BOG GARDEN

The permanently moist conditions of a bog garden provide the ideal environment for a wide range of plants. A bog garden does not have to be very large to be effective, but it does need to look as natural as possible, which means planting in drifts, rather than in straight lines. Nor does it have to go beside a pond: It can go anywhere in the garden, although it will look more natural alongside a stretch of water.

GROUND WORK

If there is an area of ground in your garden – either beside the pond or elsewhere – where the soil is heavy and constantly damp, you will be able to grow bog plants without any additional preparation. Usually, however, some preparatory work will be necessary to create the right conditions for a bog garden.

If you are siting your bog garden next to the pond, it should be constructed at the same time as the pond, using the same sheet of liner.

DRIFTS OF COLOR
Plants grow vigorously in the moist conditions of a bog garden. For maximum impact, plant bold drifts of contrasting foliage and flowers.

MAKING A BOG GARDEN

■ Dig a shallow basin about 12 in (30 cm) deep. Keep the topsoil, as this can be used later. Line the basin with a 2-in (5-cm) layer of sand.

■ Lay a sheet of flexible liner over the sand. If the bog garden is adjacent to the pond, continue the liner from the pond across the excavated area. It is, however, essential that you create a watertight barrier between the pond and the boggy extension; otherwise the plants in the bog garden will take the water they need from the pond, causing the level to drop rapidly in periods of hot weather. To avoid this, bring the liner up above the surface and cement stones or rocks directly onto it so no water can seep through.

PLANTING A BOG GARDEN

■ Puncture holes in the liner for drainage – one ½-in (13-mm) hole every 3 ft (90 cm) should be enough to ensure that the water in the bog garden is free-draining and moisture-retentive but not waterlogged.

■ Cover the liner with a 2-in (5-cm) layer of washed gravel.

■ Add the soil on top of the gravel, keeping the level below that of the pond. A good mix would be 3 parts topsoil (from the excavation), 3 parts peat, and 1 part lime-free grit.

■ Trim the liner around the edges and cover beneath 3 in (7 cm) of soil.

■ Plant directly into the soil. Plants will grow vigorously in the wet conditions so avoid invasive species.

■ You may consider adding leaf mold or an organic fertilizer – but only if there is no danger of leaching into the pond.

PLANT CHOICE

Among the most popular plants for a bog garden are feathery red, pink, white, and cream astilbes, handsome-leaved hostas, irises, such as Japanese iris *(Iris ensata)* and *I. siberica*, and *Lobelia cardinalis* with bright red foliage and flowers. Not all primulas are suited to a bog garden, and those that are, like some shade. Good choices are the purple-blue drumstick primula *(Primula denticulata)* and the yellow bog primula *(P. florindae)*, which grows to 3 ft (90 cm). For more choices and plant descriptions, turn to pages 108–111. Also look at marginals on pages 102–105, many of which will thrive in a bog garden.

CANDELABRA PRIMULA

4

ATTRACTING WILDLIFE

Within a very short space of time, a new pond, irrespective of whether or not it has been specifically designed with wildlife in mind, will be teeming with various inhabitants. Most of these will be beneficial, just the occasional pest will need to be rooted out.

AMPHIBIANS

Frogs, toads, and newts will soon discover and enter a new pond to breed and, once established, will return each year. Feeding on garden pests, such as slugs, these small amphibians are of great benefit in the garden and should be encouraged.

To enable amphibians to climb in and out of the pond, create ramps by placing short wooden planks or flat stones between the edge of the water and dry land.

EASY ACCESS
A few rocks sloping from the edge into the water provide wildlife with access to the pond – frogs to spawn and breed, and birds to bathe.

■ **Frogs** Female common frogs lay their spawn in jelly-like clumps in early spring, soon after they emerge from their winter hibernation. About a week later, the tadpoles hatch and start feeding on algae. Although to begin with, there will be hundreds of tadpoles – each female lays between 2,000 and 4,000 eggs – if there are fish in the same pond, few survive. Birds and newts, as well as damselfly and dragonfly nymphs, will also reduce their numbers. As tadpoles can also be cannibalistic, only the strongest will survive to develop legs and leave the pond as froglets some 12 weeks after hatching.

4

Although frogs must return to a pond to breed, they spend most of their life in long grass, flower beds, and other damp places on land. In summer you will often see them around the pond, sunning themselves on a lily pad or clinging to the sides cooling off, half in and half out of the water. In winter they hibernate under logs and stones.

■ **Toads** Female common toads prefer bigger ponds and lay their eggs in ribbons, some 10–12 ft (3–4 m) long, entwined around water plants. Toads are generally larger than frogs, have a drier, more warty skin, and hop or walk rather than leap. They often live well away from water and may stay in one locality for a long time. Toads feed at night on slugs and worms or small insects caught on their sticky, extendible tongue.

■ **Newts** These small lizard-like amphibians spend part of their life in water. The two most common species are the common or smooth newt and the great crested or warty newt. Like frogs and toads they lay spawn in spring, which hatch into tadpoles. After breeding, the adults leave the water and live under damp stones.

SNAILS AND MUSSELS

The only safe snail to introduce to a garden pond is the ramshorn snail, which feeds off scraps of decaying matter. The eggs that they produce provide a tasty treat for fish, but although they will also feed on algae, they are not really necessary in a garden pond. Never give the great pond snail a home, or they will tear your waterlily leaves to shreds and decimate other water plants. These snails will also eat frog spawn.

Swan mussels are sometimes sold to filter out microscopic algae, but they are of little value in a pond that does not have a muddy bottom.

RESIDENT TOAD
Toads spend most of their life in the garden – keeping down unwelcome slugs – but every spring they must return to a pond to breed.

INSECT LIFE

On warm spring and summer days you will often see dragonflies and the more delicate damselflies flitting and hovering over the water's surface in search of insect prey or a mate. Both are fierce predators, feeding on smaller insects that they have captured in flight or snatched from pondside vegetation.

Dragonflies and damselflies are the adult forms of larvae, or nymphs, that have spent the previous year under water, foraging for food, such as newly hatched tadpoles. When they are mature, the nymphs pull themselves out of the water by climbing up the nearby stems of marginal plants.

It doesn't take pondskaters, with their long, thin legs much time to find a new stretch of water on which to settle. They may be joined on the surface by water crickets, water measurers, and whirligig beetles. If you keep fish, two underwater insects to remove from your pond are water boatmen and great diving beetles, both of which are large enough to nip at small fish, often resulting in bacterial infection setting in. The larvae of great diving beetles will also attack very young fish and tadpoles, as will pondskaters and water boatmen. All aquatic insects are good fliers, so keep a regular watch for any new arrivals.

LESS WELCOME VISITORS

Birds will visit a garden pond to drink and bathe, and also to feed on tiny flies and mosquitoes that gather there. One bird you don't want to see, if you have fish, is a heron. You may not even see one as they tend to arrive at dawn or dusk, and will even visit urban ponds in search of a tasty meal.

PLASTIC HERON DECOY

These birds do not go directly to a pond, but land nearby, and wade in; so the more open your pond, the more vulnerable it may be, particularly the shallow areas. If herons are a problem, a plastic heron decoy is said to keep the real thing away, or the pond could be netted. A less unsightly method is to wrap two strands of wire or fishing line around 6-in (15-m) stakes positioned about 1 ft (30 cm) around the edge of the pond.

Cats, particularly kittens, may take an interest in your pond, but they don't really like water, and in any case healthy fish would normally be too quick for their probing paws.

Mink and even otters have been known to take fish from a garden pond, and if these, or herons and cats are a real nuisance you could invest in an infrared sensor unit to warn them off. These emit a high-pitched alarm when a warm-blooded animal or bird strays into the area.

4

Pond care and maintenance

5

Pond care and maintenance

Many people worry unduly that the aftercare needed for a healthy pond involves endless time-consuming maintenance tasks, and so they are deterred from installing a water feature in their gardens. This is a shame, as looking after a pond is more often than not an easy and rewarding occupation. Throughout the year it is important to remove all dead and dying organic matter, such as leaves, from the pond. Other tasks are more seasonal. This chapter looks in greater detail at basic pond management, from the tools and equipment you will need to how to completely drain the pond when it needs cleaning. A checklist of routine jobs explains what needs doing and when.

The chapter finishes off with a troubleshooter's guide to problems that can arise in a pond, and suggests how you can remedy them.

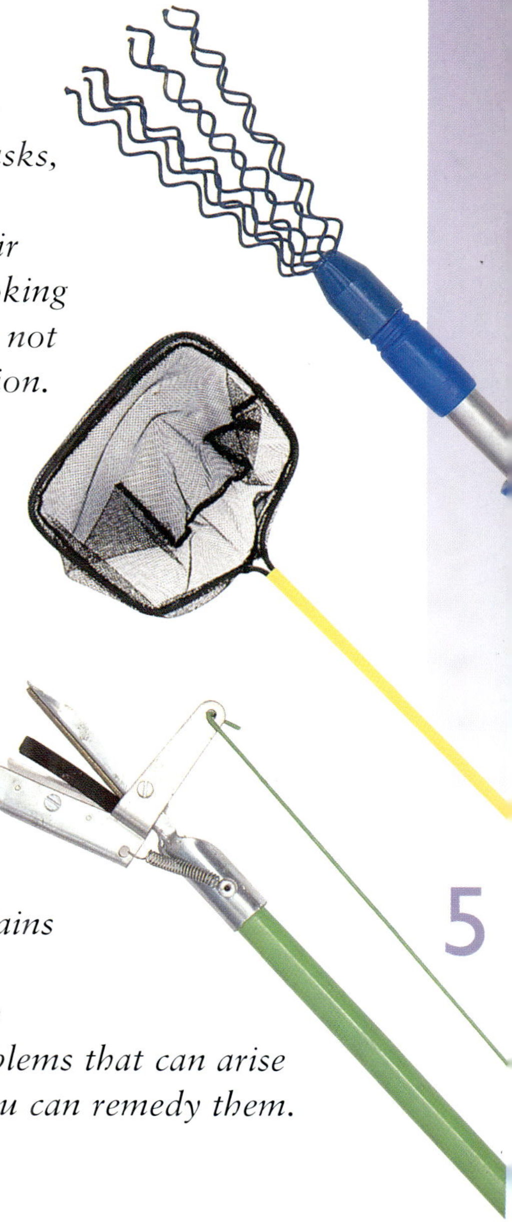

5

ROUTINE CARE

Looking after a pond could not be easier. Aquatic plants do not need watering, and fish only need feeding when they are active. In order to prevent problems occurring, however, there are a few routine jobs that must be done, such as removing dead and dying plants, fallen leaves, blanketweed, and dead fish. The water level should also be checked to ensure that this does not fluctuate. Make sure that electrical equipment, such as pumps and filters, are regularly serviced.

BASIC EQUIPMENT

- **Pond skimmer** A rake, fork, or specially designed pond skimmer can be used to remove blanketweed.
- **Pond scissors** Long-handled, cable-operated pond scissors are used to trim out-of-reach aquatic plants.
- **Pond pincers** Cable-operated pond pincers are used to remove debris from the surface.
- **Garden hose** A good-quality hose is essential for keeping the water level topped up.

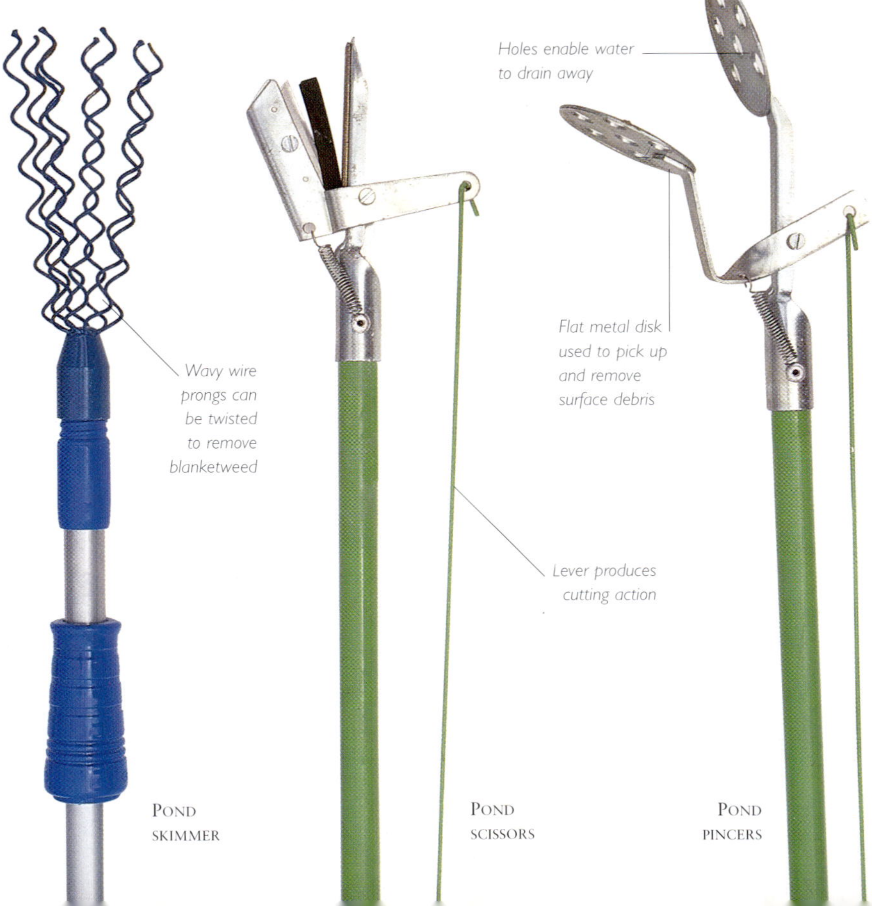

POND SKIMMER

POND SCISSORS

POND PINCERS

5

■ **Scrub brush** A hard-bristled scrub brush is essential for cleaning off algae. Remember never to use detergent for cleaning.

■ **Fishing nets** Long-handled fishing nets in different sizes are useful for lifting out fish.

SPRING CLEANING

It is neither necessary nor desirable to change the water in your pond too frequently. If properly stocked with plants and fish, the balance of the pond should remain healthy and it is usually sufficient to remove about a quarter of the water and replace it with fresh once a year.

However, every two to three years (less frequently for a large pond) you will need to empty the pond in order to thin out overcrowded waterlilies and marginals and remove debris that has built up on the bottom. The best time to tackle this is early to mid-spring.

Before cleaning the pond, take care to avoid harming any wildlife that may have taken up residence. If your pond is home to frogs or toads, you will have to postpone any cleanup until mid-fall as there will be spawn and young in the spring.

DRAINING THE POND

Every few years, you will need to drain your pond to remove silt, debris, overcrowded plants – or fix a leak. Wear rubber boots or waders with cleated soles that will not damage the pond liner.

■ **Start emptying** Use a length of hose to begin siphoning away the water. Alternatively, if you have a pump, simply disconnect the delivery pipe and connect a hose in its place.

■ **Catch fish** Fill a large plastic holding tub or children's paddling pool with pond water and use it to place the fish in while you clean out the pond. As the water slowly drains away, catch the fish (see p. 70) with a net and place them in the holding tub. Cover the tub with netting so they cannot jump out and leave it in the shade. Keep any amphibians in a bucket filled with pond water.

■ **Remove plants** As the water drains away, remove all containerized plants. Marginals and deep-water aquatics will need to be hosed down frequently to keep them wet. Floaters and oxygenators can be kept in plastic containers filled with water.

FINE-MESH FISHING NET

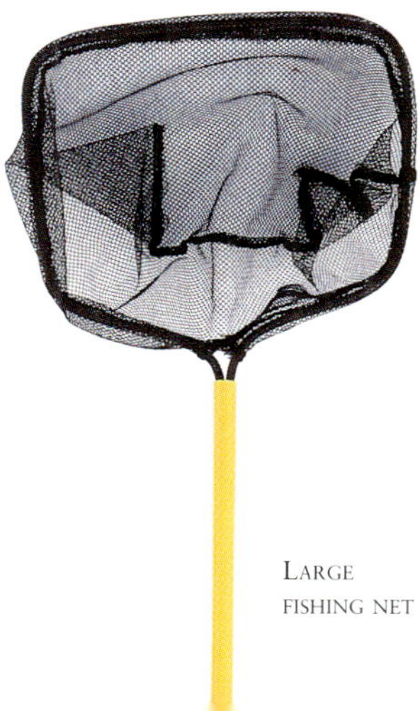

LARGE FISHING NET

SMALL FISHING NET

Cleaning the pond

Once the pond is drained, allow it to dry for a couple of days.

■ **Remove sludge** Use a bucket to remove sludge; spread it on a border.

■ **Wash liner** A pressure hose will remove most algal growth. Use a soft broom to sweep up debris.

■ **Refill pond** Use a hose to start refilling the pond.

■ **Replace plants** Divide plants as necessary and clean out containers. Position ornamental plants first, then add submerged plants.

■ **Replace fish** Acclimatize the fish (see p. 69) before putting them back.

BRUSHING DOWN
Use a soft broom and dustpan to sweep up any debris, taking great care not to damage the fabric of the liner. Do not use any detergent.

Seasonal care

Throughout the year, as the temperature changes from season to season, so will the conditions in your pond. By being aware of the problems you could potentially face and carrying out routine seasonal tasks, you will be able to maintain a healthy balance in your pond.

Spring

As the water temperature rises, plants begin to shoot, fish become more active, and spawn soon appears.

■ **Check pump** Bring the pump out of winter storage, check the wiring, and reinstall in the pond.

■ **Fish** Resume feeding the fish (see pp. 70–71) once temperatures rise. Check for disease (see p. 91).

REMOVING BLANKETWEED
It is essential to remove blanketweed from the pond as soon as you notice it, or it will quickly start to choke all other plant and animal life.

■ **Remove algae** Use a pond skimmer or rake to remove all algae.

■ **Tidy plants** Lift and divide overcrowded aquatics in late spring; inspect containers for stray roots, which can be cut off.

■ **Feed plants** Feed established plants in late spring. Push pellets of aquatic plant fertilizer into the soil in each individual plant container.

■ **Add new plants** Add oxygenators to inhibit algal growth and floating plants to provide surface shade.

Summer

At this time of year, your pond will be looking its best. The irises will come into flower, followed by water-lilies and marginals, such as lobelia.

■ **Feed fish** Now the fish are at their most active and should be fed daily.

■ **Spray plants** Occasionally spray the leaves of marginals and water-lilies with water from a hose or a can to dislodge insects, such as blackfly.

■ **Add new fish** Higher water temperatures make this the best time to introduce new fish into the pond.

■ **Top up water level** Using a hose, regularly replace water lost through evaporation.

■ **Oxygenate water** In warm, humid weather, keep the fountain running – all night if necessary – or spray the surface of the water with a hose. This increases the oxygen level – vital for fish and plant life – and lowers its carbon dioxide content.

■ **Deadhead flowers** Remove dead flowers before they set seed and trim back overvigorous marginals.

■ **Skim pond** Remove pondweed and blanketweed by winding it around a stick or fork.

■ **Clean pumps and filters** Pumps and filters will need regular cleaning to prevent their being blocked by weed and other debris.

Spraying leaves removes colonies of insects

Fall

As plants begin to fade, it is important to deal immediately with dead and dying matter and not let it fall and rot in the water.

■ **Catch leaves** Place a fine mesh net, such as strawberry netting, over the pond surface to catch falling leaves. It is easier to keep leaves out than to remove them after they have fallen in.

■ **Remove debris** Use a pond skimmer, rake, or fishing net to remove dead leaves and other debris.

■ **Deadhead flowers** Remove faded flowers and dead leaves from waterlilies and other floating plants.

■ **Cut back plants** Once leaves and stems have turned brown, cut marginals down to about 3–4 in (7–10 cm) above the water line. This will remove any foliage pests.

■ **Prepare plants for winter** Before temperatures drop below freezing, remove any non-hardy aquatics and some of the floating plants to overwinter indoors. They should be kept in shallow bowls of water at a temperature of 50–55°F (10–13°C). The remaining floating plants – which will survive in the water during winter – can be left to sink to the bottom of the pond.

■ **Prepare fish for winter** Give fish a food high in protein to build up their strength for the winter. Put a few lengths of plastic guttering in the bottom of the pond, to give them somewhere to shelter once the cover offered by floating plants is no longer available.

■ **Remove the pump** Clean the pump and store it in a dry place over winter. Replace it with a pond heater.

Cutting back marginals

5

WINTER

Besides preventing the pond surface from freezing over, there is little work to be done in the pond during the winter. The fish will be semi-dormant, remaining close to the bottom, and should not be fed.

■ **Deice the pond** In very cold climates, a pond heater is the best way of keeping an area of water ice-free. This should be installed in the fall before temperatures drop below freezing and can be connected to the electricity supply that powered the pump.

In warmer climates, place a floating object, such as a rubber ball, on the surface to prevent the pond from freezing over. This allows the gases produced by decaying matter to escape. These gases are toxic and may kill the fish. Never crack the ice with a hammer, as the shock waves can concuss or even kill fish.

If there is no power supply to the pond, a pan of boiling water placed on the ice will melt a hole. You will need to do this perhaps several times a day if the weather is really cold. Never pour the boiling water into the pond as the shock may harm the fish.

■ **Year-round algal control** Fully biodegradable straw pads are now available to float in your pond. Not only do they keep down algae, they will prevent the pond from freezing over. Each pad will usually last for about six months.

BIODEGRADABLE STRAW PADS FOR CONTROLLING ALGAE

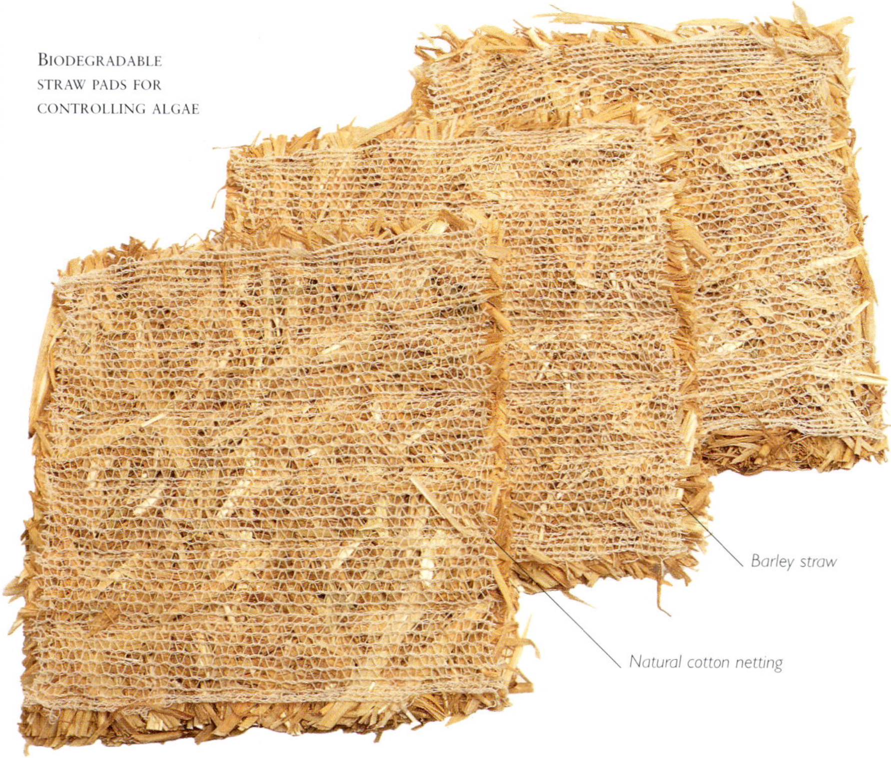

5

POND TROUBLESHOOTER

If you build and stock your pond correctly, carry out routine maintenance, avoid the unnecessary use of chemicals, and keep a close watch on your plants and fish; owning a pond should not give you too many problems. Very few pests and diseases attack aquatic plants, and if fish are well cared for, they should not succumb to ailments. There will, however, be occasions when a plant gets eaten, a fish looks off color, or the water becomes polluted.

PLANT PROBLEMS

Aquatic plants suffer from few serious pest and disease problems – which is just as well because the risk of polluting the pond water means that chemicals and sprays cannot be used as in other parts of the garden. The only spray that can be used is that from a hose to wash off insects, such as aphids, from a waterlily leaf.

One of the simplest and most efficient methods of controlling pests and diseases is to remove the affected leaf, or plant, as soon as you notice a problem.

Natural predators, such as frogs, newts, and ladybugs, as well as fish, will also play their part in helping to keep pest populations under control.

PLANT PESTS AND DISEASES

Caddis fly larvae
Mothlike adult caddis flies visit ponds on summer evenings to lay their eggs on floating leaves. When the eggs hatch, the larvae attack and feed on the roots, leaves, and buds of all aquatic plants, particularly young waterlilies. They spin cylindrical silken shelters, which they disguise with pieces of plant, sticks, and grit. The best way of reducing their numbers is to introduce fish into the pond, which will soon make a meal of them. Remove any larval cases by hand.

Iris sawfly
This blue-gray grub, about ¾ in (2 cm) long, feeds on irises. Signs of damage are ragged or saw-toothed edges on the leaves, which should be removed, along with any grubs, and destroyed.

Leaf-mining midge
This midge lays its eggs on a wide range of soft-leaved aquatics, including waterlilies. The almost invisible larvae tunnel into the leaf, rapidly devouring the tissue between the veins, leaving a partially, or in some cases totally skeletonized leaf. Pick off affected foliage.

China mark moth
These brown and white moths lay eggs on waterlily leaves in mid- to late summer. If left, the emerging caterpillars will cause extensive damage. They begin by biting oval-shaped pieces out of the leaf and spinning two pieces together to form a shelter, which they attach to the underside of the leaf. As the caterpillars grow, they cut larger pieces of leaf to form a protective oblong case that floats on the water – with the caterpillar safely inside. Remove these cases using a small net and destroy them.

PLANT PESTS AND DISEASES

Water snails
You can often introduce water snails into your pond on the leaves of newly purchased aquatics. Although they can be beneficial, eating both algae and fish waste as well as dead and dying plant matter, they can become a pest, particularly in spring when they may turn their attention to more succulent fresh plant growth. They should be removed with a fish net.

Garden snails
The lush growth of marginals around the edge of a pond will attract garden snails, which should be picked off by hand. It would also be a good idea to place a couple of slug traps in the vicinity. Some hollowed-out potato skins or a half-filled jar of beer sunk into the ground work well. Never use slug pellets.

Waterlily aphid
In hot, dry weather, waterlily leaves, stems, and flowers may become infested by aphids, weakening the plant and distorting both flowers and foliage. Dislodge the aphids by spraying with a jet of water from a garden hose. Alternatively, submerge the leaves and weight them down with a piece of sacking to drown the aphids.

In the fall, these aphids leave the pond to lay eggs on trees and shrubs of the *Prunus* genus. To reduce the chances of infestation, avoid siting the pond near a cherry or plum tree.

Waterlily beetle
The small brown adult beetle, the size of a ladybug, lays its eggs in clusters on the upper surface of waterlily leaves in midsummer. The yellowish brown grubs that emerge have a voracious appetite, mining the leaves, which shrivel and rot. Remove badly affected leaves, and hose down the rest. Cut down dead stalks of marginals in the fall, as this is where the lily beetle likes to hibernate.

Waterlily crown rot
Crown rot attacks the stem of the waterlily, causing the leaves to turn yellow and break away. As there is no cure, the only course of action is to remove and destroy the infected plant. If other plants have been infected, the pond will have to be emptied, thoroughly cleaned, and restocked. To guard against this disease, before planting waterlilies, inspect the rhizomes carefully. Reject any that have a black and soft area.

Waterlily leaf spot
Leaf spot is triggered by a prolonged spell of warm, damp weather. Two forms attack waterlily pads: the leaves either dry out and disintegrate, or a dark spot forms, which spreads and destroys the whole leaf. To stop the infection from spreading, remove diseased leaves immediately.

Check waterlilies regularly for pests and diseases

5

FISH

Fish are at their most vulnerable to disease and parasite attack in early spring and after the spawning season. After a long winter, or if you suspect a problem, you may want to take a closer look at your fish. To do this, each one will need to be caught and transferred into a tank of water at the same temperature as that of the pond (see p. 69). Don't chase the fish around the pond, as this will exhaust them. Take it slowly and carefully. Before handling fish (see p. 70), make sure your hands are wet so you don't strip off their protective mucous coat. Keep any affected fish in an isolation tank until fully recovered. Treatments such as bactericides and fungicides are available; always read the manufacturer's instructions first.

COMMON FISH AILMENTS

Fin rot
This is a fairly common bacterial disease that destroys the bony rays of the tail fin, particularly of long-finned goldfish and shubunkins. If allowed to progress, fin rot will eventually reach other parts of the body, resulting in the death of the fish. The treatment is to cut away the infected area with a pair of scissors and place the fish in a solution of approved bactericide. The tail fin will regrow once the infection is cleared.

Fungus
A cottonlike growth on the fins, gills, eyes, and mouth of a fish is a sign of a fungus, which attacks a debilitated fish whose protective mucous membrane has been damaged by stress, spawning, or temperature change. Fungus can be successfully treated by using a suitable fungicide.

White spot
If a fish is seen swimming frenziedly, and looks as if it has been sprinkled with salt, it has been infected by a small parasite. Treat affected fish as soon as you notice the problem with a proprietary remedy. Do not confuse this disease with the white spots that will quite normally appear on the gills of male fish during the mating season.

Fish lice
Each fish louse is a jelly-like disk, about ¼ in (6 mm) across, which attaches itself to the body of a fish to feed off its blood. It will cause a fish to rub itself against the side of the pond and swim rapidly around. Treatment involves either removing the lice with tweezers or applying an appropriate remedy. You will need to repeat the treatment as even after you have eliminated the adult lice, there may still be eggs in the water.

Ulcer disease
Shredded fins and ulcers on the body indicates the onset of ulcer disease, which affects all types of fish. Treatment does, however, require antibiotics, which should be administered under the guidance of a vet.

KEEP AN EYE ON FISH FOR ANY SIGNS OF DISEASE

5

WATER

Keeping the water in the pond clean and well oxygenated is essential for the health of fish and plants. Carry out routine tasks such as skimming leaves and debris from the surface and removing blanketweed as soon as it appears. Never use garden fertilizers in or around the pond.

KEEPING WATER CLEAN

ALGAE

In small quantities algae is beneficial to the pond and provides food for fish. However, excess growth will turn the water green, indicating that the pond balance is not quite right. To create a better balance try the following:

- Introduce more oxygenating plants, and provide surface shade using waterlilies and other floating plants.
- Until the oxygenators are established and the water stays clear, skim off algae once a week.
- You can use an algicide, but always read the instructions carefully first.
- A nonchemical solution to algae is a bag of barley straw weighted down on the bottom of the pond or a floating, biodegradable pad (see p. 88).
- If fighting algae is a constant battle, install a filter for a more permanent solution.

INVASIVE PLANTS

- **Blanketweed** The scourge of pondkeepers everywhere, the long, silky green threads of blanketweed (a form of algae) choke other plants and hide fish from view. Remove the weed by winding it around a stick and put it on the compost heap. Treat the water with an algicide.
- **Duckweed** Never introduce duckweed into your pond. Before long the surface will be covered by its tiny green leaves, and as it is hardy it is almost impossible to completely eradicate. Remove as much as you can using a net before it gets out of control and check the pots of aquatics when you buy them to see that they don't contain any of this unwanted plant.
- **Fairy moss** Once introduced, fairy moss, also called water fern *(Azolla filiculoides,* syn. *A. caroliniana),* can quickly get out of hand, particularly in a small pond.

POLLUTION

Water pollution is harmful to fish and to plants and can manifest itself in several ways:

- An oily film on the surface could be due to the decomposition of waterlily leaves and other deep-water aquatic foliage. This film can be mopped up by placing a sheet of newspaper on the surface.
- Black water is the result of rotting leaves in the water. In severe cases, the pond may need to be drained and cleaned. Note that brown, or muddy water, although unsightly, is harmless to fish and plants. In fact, it is probably the fish who are to blame, stirring up soil in plant containers or on the bottom as they scavenge for food.
- Never use any kind of manure, fertilizer, or chemical weed-killer in or around the pond as this will eventually find its way into the water. The only solution is draining and cleaning.

Plant directory

PLANT DIRECTORY

Plants are essential for an attractive and successful water garden, bringing life and color to even the smallest feature.

While oxygenators and many floating plants serve a practical purpose, helping to maintain a healthy balance in the pond, many marginals are valued simply for their beautiful colors, forms, and texture, softening the hard edges of an ornamental pond and helping it to blend in with the rest of the garden.

This chapter looks at some of the most popular plants from the five categories: waterlilies, floating plants, deep-water aquatics, marginals, and oxygenators, together with some ideas for plants that can be used around the pond and in a bog garden.

WATERLILIES

There are as many as 16,000 varieties of waterlily *(Nymphaea)*, which must rank as the most popular of all pond plants. There are varieties to suit all sizes and depths of a pond, but all need sun, shelter, and still water to thrive. Take care to thin out overcrowded plants.

SMALL VARIETIES

The following varieties are all suitable for small ponds. They require a planting depth of 6–18 in (15–45 cm) and will spread 1–2 ft (30–60 cm).

N. 'Andreana'
The brick-red flowers, held above the water, are shaded with yellow, with rich orange stamens. The leaves are glossy green blotched with red.

N. 'Aurora'
Semi-double flowers in a wide range of shades deepening from cream to yellow, orange, and blood-red, with orange stamens. Olive-green leaves mottled with purple.

N. candida
A small variety with pure white flowers that thrives even in relatively cold water. Mid-green leaves.

N. 'Ellisiana'
Star-shaped, fragrant, bright red flowers, with orange-red stamens. The oval leaves are dark green mottled with purple when young, maturing to mid-green.

N. 'Firecrest'
Semi-double, star-shaped, pink flowers have orange stamens. The deep purple young leaves mature to mid-green.

N. 'Froebelii'
Deep red flowers with orange-red stamens. Bronzed young leaves mature to pale green.

N. 'Gloriosa'
The brilliant red, cup-shaped flowers, have rose and green variegated sepals. The green leaves have bronzy flecks.

N. 'Graziella'
A free-flowering pinkish orange waterlily, suitable for the smallest of ponds.

N. 'James Brydon'
Double, rose-red flowers with orange stamens. The young leaves are purple, maturing to dark green. Tolerates some shade.

N. 'Odorata Sulphurea'
The sulfur-yellow flowers with orange stamens are carried above the water. Performs best in a warm summer.

N. 'Pygmaea Helvola'
Small, semi-double flowers are a clear buttercup yellow. Oval, mottled purple leaves with purple undersides.

N. 'Rose Arey'
A free-flowering variety with star-shaped, semi-double, anise-scented flowers, deep rose-pink when young, becoming paler with age. The young leaves are purple, maturing to green.

N. 'Sioux'
The pointed petals start off a pale yellow, deepening to an orange-pink before finally turning a copper red. The dark olive green leaves are mottled with purple.

N. tetragona
Small, day-blooming, slightly scented white flowers with dark green, purple-blotched leaves.

N.'Virginalis'
Star-shaped, fragrant white flowers with yellow stamens. Rounded, pale green leaves, purplish when young.

VIGOROUS VARIETIES

The following varieties are only suitable for a large pond or lake. They require a planting depth of 1–4 ft (30–120 cm) and will spread 5–8 ft 1.5–2.4 m).

N. alba
Common white waterlily
Slightly fragrant white flowers with yellow stamens. Large, rounded, dark green leaves. Very vigorous.

***N.* 'Amabilis'**
Star-shaped pink flowers with white tips and dark yellow stamens. The dark green leaves are reddish purple when young.

***N.* 'Brakeleyi Rosea'**
The fragrant, shell-pink flowers with golden stamens are held just above the surface of the water. Large green lily pads give plenty of surface cover.

N. capensis
Cape blue waterlily
This tropical waterlily will not survive below 41°F (5°C) but can be grown as an annual in cool climates. Semi-double, star-shaped, fragrant, light blue flowers with dark yellow stamens. The young leaves have wavy edges and purple-spotted undersides.

***N.* 'Charles de Meurville'**
Star-shaped, pinkish red, white-streaked flowers that darken with age and have golden stamens. Flowers appear early. Oval, dark green leaves.

***N.* 'Colonel A. J. Welch'**
A vigorous variety with large, canary-yellow flowers that stand out of the water and stay open in the evening. The leaves have a marbled effect.

***N.* 'Colossea'**
A strong-growing variety requiring a planting depth of 5 ft (1.5 m). The large blush-pink to white blooms are fragrant and borne over a long period.

***N.* 'Darwin'**
Large, dark pink flowers striped with white and scented. The stamens are golden.

***N.* 'Escarboucle'**
Prolific, fragrant, semi-double, rich red blooms with golden stamens. The young leaves are brown tinged, maturing to green.

***N.* 'Fabiola' syn. *N.* 'Mrs Richmond'**
The inner petals of this pink waterlily turn red with age, while the leaves are a paler green than most. Very prolific.

***N.* 'Gladstoneana'**
Semi-double, pure white fragrant flowers with golden stamens, reaching up to 12 in (30 cm) across. The leaves have a wavy edge to them. Very free-flowering.

***N.* 'Norma Gedye'**
Deep rose-pink flowers and plain, dark green leaves.

N. 'COLONEL A. J. WELCH'

MEDIUM VARIETIES

The following varieties are all suitable for medium to large ponds. They require a planting depth of 9–24 in (15–60 cm) and will spread 4–5 ft (1.2–1.5 m).

N. 'Attraction'
Mature plants have large, star-shaped, red flowers flecked with white, while the flowers on younger plants are smaller, cup-shaped and pale pink. The stamens are pale yellow. When young, the leaves are purple, maturing to green.

N. 'Carolineana Nivea'
The large, semi-double, ivory-white flowers are strongly fragrant with yellow stamens. The pale green leaves are rounded.

N. 'Conqueror'
An eye-catching, free-flowering brilliant red waterlily. The large flowers, which are sometimes flecked with white, stay open in the evening. The young leaves are tinged with purple.

N. 'Gonnère'
The multi-petaled white flower looks like a snowball before it opens to reveal a bright yellow center. Its more restrained spread makes it suitable for a medium-sized pond.

N. 'Hermine'
The pure white flowers with their pointed petals are held well above the water. The pads are a bright green.

N. 'Laydekeri Fulgens'
Free-flowering blooms through summer. Semi-double burgundy-red flowers have orange-red stamens. The young leaves are blotched with purple.

N. 'Lucida'
Bright scarlet flowers with bright yellow stamens and large leaves with purple marbling make this an attractive waterlily for a medium to large pond.

N. 'Mme Wilfon Gonnère'
Cup-shaped double blooms, soft pink flushed with white with a deep rose center and yellow stamens. Mid-green leaves are bronze when young.

N. 'Marliacea Albida'
Fragrant, cup-shaped white flowers with yellow stamens. The young, bronzed leaves mature to dark green.

N. 'Marliacea Chromatella'
Cup-shaped, semi-double golden yellow flowers set off against mottled bronze and maroon leaves. A reliable performer.

N. 'Marliacea Chromatella'

MEDIUM VARIETIES

***N.* 'Marliacea Rosea'**
With its pink, fragrant flowers and golden stamens, this is an easy waterlily to grow and very popular. The large, fragrant blooms darken with age. Flowers produced in the first few years may be white. The dark green leaves are purplish when young.
• *N.* 'Marliacea Carnea' is similar in appearance but the flowers are just a slightly paler pink.

***N.* 'Masaniello'**
Peony-like, rose-pink flowers with darker petals at the center, standing above the surface of the water.

***N.* 'Nigel'**
This waterlily produces a mass of bright pink flowers with golden stamens, set off against large green leaves.

N. odorata
Cup- or star-shaped, fragrant white flowers with yellow stamens and glossy mid-green leaves.
• *N. o.* var. *rosea* is similar but has pink flowers.

***N.* 'Pearl of the Pool'**
Large, star-shaped, bright pink flowers have orange stamens and are fragrant. The leaves are bronzed when young, maturing to mid-green.

***N.* 'Perry's Pink'**
The deep pink, large double flowers with red centers are fragrant. Needs a lot of sunshine to do well.

***N.* 'Pink Sensation'**
Fragrant, rich pink, star-shaped flowers are held above the water and stay open late into the afternoon. Leaves are purplish when young, maturing to deep green.

***N.* 'René Gérard'**
This waterlily has distinctive upright and star-shaped, rose-pink flowers. The young leaves are bronzed, maturing to mid-green. Very free-flowering once established.

N. 'PINK SENSATION'

***N.* 'Robinsoniana'**
Star-shaped, orange-red flowers with orange stamens. The leaves are light purple, with deep purple blotches and dark red undersides. Very free-flowering once established.

***N.* 'Sunrise'**
Semi-double flowers with long yellow petals and yellow stamens. The oval leaves are mottled with purple when young, maturing to mid-green. Needs warm summers.

***N.* 'William Falconer'**
A stunning deep red waterlily with dark yellow stamens. The flowers are star-shaped. The young leaves are purple but mature to dark green.

FLOATING PLANTS

It is important to introduce one or two floating aquatics to your pond as they cut down the amount of sunlight on the surface of the water and so help control blanketweed and green algae that can pollute the water. Most floating plants have attractive flowers and/or leaves, although the most attractive are usually the least hardy, and will need to be overwintered indoors.

SURFACE INTEREST

Floating plants often multiply rapidly and their growth must be constantly controlled. Some, such as water hyacinth *(Eichhornia crassipes),* while not invasive in temperate areas are so vigorous in tropical climates that their introduction may be prohibited. In areas with cold winters most floaters are killed as soon as temperatures drop below freezing. Where they are hardy, plants sink to the bottom in winter and float back to the surface in spring.

■ **Warning** Although it may provide food and shelter for fish, *Lemna,* or duckweed, should never be knowingly introduced into a garden pond. You may have seen it in stagnant ponds – a bright green blanket covering the surface. Once you have duckweed, it will be virtually impossible to eradicate.

Take care, also, when introducing other plants to your pond that there is no duckweed lurking in the water or on the plant itself.

ORIENTAL WATER GARDEN

FLOATING AQUATICS

Azolla filiculoides*, syn. *Azolla caroliniana
Fairy moss, water fern
This plant's dense mat of pale green, fernlike foliage will quickly spread to cover the whole surface, so only put it in a pond where it can easily be removed. In late summer and fall, the fronds turn reddish. It will not stand freezing temperatures, so overwinter some in a jar of pond water and soil, and put it back into the pond in mid-spring.

Eichornia crassipes
Water hyacinth
This attractive aquatic has glossy leaves and feathery roots. However, the orchidlike lilac blue flower spikes will only appear in a warm, sunny summer: in cooler, duller conditions it may not flower. Plant out in early summer, but take inside before the first frost as it is a tender plant.

Hydrocharis morsus ranae
Frogbit
With its shiny, kidney-shaped, bright olive-green leaves and small white flowers in summer, frogbit resembles a miniature waterlily. It dies down to small buds to overwinter on the bottom of the pond. A must for a natural pond as it is a favorite haunt for aquatic wildlife. Divide in summer, by detaching young plantlets.

Pistia stratiotes
Water lettuce
This plant's common name comes from its velvety, pale green, lettucelike leaves, which are whitish green on the underside. The flowers are tiny and greenish. Thin and separate new plantlets in summer. It will not tolerate winter cold, but can be grown as an annual in cool climates.

Stratiotes aloides
Water soldier
This unusual plant spends most of its life submerged, only coming to the surface at flowering time, when white, three-petaled flowers are produced. The leaves are pointed and serrated, and look like the top of a pineapple. Once flowering is over, it sinks to the bottom and overwinters there as dormant buds. It needs deep water and can become invasive when conditions are favorable.

Trapa natans
Water chestnut
This attractive plant with floating rosettes of diamond-shaped, green serrated leaves gets its common name from the black spiny "nuts" that follow the flowers in summer. These fall to the bottom of the pond where they overwinter and produce new plants in spring. However, it will only produce its small white flower, and its fruit, in a really warm summer and will not tolerate frost.

WATER CHESTNUTS

DEEP-WATER AQUATICS

With their roots on the bottom and leaves floating on the surface, deep-water aquatics provide shade to prevent the growth of algae. Plant in containers on bricks a few inches (centimeters) under the water and gradually lower as the plants become established.

DEEP-WATER AQUATICS

Aponogeton distachyos
Water hawthorn
This is an easy plant to grow and probably one of the most reliable deep-water aquatics. The straplike leaves are often evergreen and are sometimes splashed with purple. The flowers appear throughout spring and early summer. These are borne on spikes that rise above the surface, and each has waxy white petals and black anthers and a heavy scent of "vanilla" or "hawthorn." Unlike a waterlily, water hawthorn will flourish in partial shade and moving water, but in winter you will need to check that the tubers are deep enough in the pond to sit below any ice that may form. The plant dies back in summer, but will bloom again through the fall and even on into winter.
PLANTING DEPTH 6–18 in (15–45 cm) – the deeper the better.
SPREAD 4 ft (1.2 m)
PROPAGATION Divide in late spring or sow fresh seed under glass. Plants will often self-seed.

NYMPHOIDES PELTATA

Nuphar
Pond lily
Although the pond lilies resemble true waterlilies, the flowers are smaller and carried above the water on thick stems in midsummer to mid-fall. They tolerate light shade and moving water.
- *N. minima (N. pumila)* has yellow flowers about 1 in (2.5 cm) across and almost translucent submerged foliage.
- *N. lutea* is similar to *N. minima* but needs a planting depth of 1–3 ft (30–60 cm).
- *N. japonica* (Japanese pond lily) has yellow, red-tinted flowers.

PLANTING DEPTH 6–18 in (15–45 cm)
SPREAD 4 ft (60 cm)
PROPAGATION Divide in late spring or summer.

Nymphoides peltata
Water fringe, floating heart
The leaves of this deciduous perennial look rather like those of a miniature waterlily and measure about 3 in (7.5 cm) across, but the dainty yellow flowers are more like those of a buttercup. These have fringed edges and are borne in small clusters about 2–3 in (5–8 cm) above the surface from midsummer to early fall. This is a useful plant for giving rapid surface cover early in the season before the true waterlilies become established, but it tends to be invasive.
PLANTING DEPTH 4–18 in (10–45 cm)
SPREAD 24 in (60 cm)
PROPAGATION Divide in late spring or summer.

DEEP-WATER AQUATICS

Orontium aquaticum
Golden club
This is a generally trouble-free, noninvasive plant, but it does need plenty of soil, so plant it in a deep, 6-in (15-cm) waterlily basket. Although it will grow in shallow water, if you want the leaves to float rather than stand erect, give it a final planting depth of at least 12 in (30 cm) of water. The leaves are blue-green with a silvery sheen, but it is the unusual flower spikes (spadix), carried in mid- to late spring and standing 1 ft (30 cm) or so above the water like gold and white pencils, that make this plant so appealing.
PLANTING DEPTH 3–12 in (7.5–30 cm)
SPREAD 24 in (60 cm)
PROPAGATION Seed sown in summer.

Polygonum amphibium
Willow grass, amphibious bistort
This perennial plant has long-stalked, floating leaves borne on stems that root at the nodes. In midsummer, pink flowers are held above the water. Will also grow in boggy margins.
PLANTING DEPTH To 18 in (45 cm)
SPREAD Indefinite
PROPAGATION By division.

Zantedeschia aethiopica
White arum
Although not fully hardy, this plant will survive the winter in most temperate areas and is well worth the risk, particularly if you have a larger pond. Look for the variety *Z. a.* 'Crowborough', which is slightly more hardy than the species. The arumlike white spathes (flowers) rise 2 ft (60 cm) or more above glossy, arrow-shaped leaves throughout the summer. In the center of each spathe is a yellow, pokerlike spadix. A few weeks later, yellow berries will appear.
PLANTING DEPTH 6–12 in (15–30 cm)
SPREAD 14–18 in (35–45 cm)
PROPAGATION Divide mature clumps in spring.

ORONTIUM AQUATICUM

MARGINALS

An attractive display of marginals at the edges of your pond will enhance its appearance and provide cover for wildlife. Although the top growth is visible above the water surface, the roots of the plants must be under water. Many will grow in bog gardens.

MARGINALS

Acorus calamus
Sweet flag
A strong-growing irislike grass with erect, swordlike leaves, which are sweetly scented when crushed.
• *A. c.* 'Variegatus' has striking cream and yellow leaves with slightly wrinkled edges.
HEIGHT 30 in (75 cm)
SPREAD 24 in (60 cm)
PLANTING DEPTH 3–5 in (7.5–15 cm)
PROPAGATION Divide overcrowded clumps in spring or summer.

Alisma plantago-aquatica
Water plantain
This attractive plant has rosettes of bright green, oval leaves held on long stalks above the water, and a profusion of small, pale pink flowers, which are produced throughout the summer. Needs frequent deadheading to stop self-sown seedlings becoming a nuisance.
HEIGHT 30 in (75 cm)
SPREAD 18 in (45 cm)
PLANTING DEPTH To 6 in (15 cm)
PROPAGATION Sow seeds or divide in summer.

Butomus umbellatus
Flowering rush, water gladiolus
An attractive aquatic, bearing a mass of rose-pink flowers in summer. These are often fragrant. The tall, narrow leaves, triangular in section, are bronze-green at first, but lose the bronze tinge as they age. Suitable for all ponds.
HEIGHT 3 ft (90 cm)
SPREAD 18 in (45 cm)
PLANTING DEPTH 3–5 in (7.5–12.5 cm), but will also grow in boggy ground.
PROPAGATION Bulbils, which are produced on the rootstock, can be planted up. Mature clumps need dividing every three years, otherwise flowering will decline.

CALTHA PALUSTRIS

Caltha palustris
Marsh marigold or Kingcup
First to bloom in the water garden, the bright golden, buttercup-like flowers are held clear of the glossy dark green leaves. Marsh marigolds look best grown in small groups at the side of the pond or in a bog garden.
• *C. p.* var. *alba* is a white variety.
• *C. p.* 'Flore Pleno' has double golden flowers. The latter two grow to 10 in (25 cm) and need a depth of 1 in (2.5 cm).
HEIGHT 24 in (60 cm)
SPREAD 18 in (45 cm)
PLANTING DEPTH To 3 in (7.5 cm)
PROPAGATION Divide overcrowded clumps in spring, or sow from seed.

MARGINALS

COTULA CORONOPIFOLIA

Cotula coronopifolia
Golden buttons

The common name comes from the small, yellow, buttonlike flowers that cover it in summer. Although short lived and treated as an annual, it does self-seed freely. Suitable for a small pond.

HEIGHT 6 in (15 cm)
SPREAD 12 in (30 cm)
PLANTING DEPTH To 5 in (12.5 cm)
PROPAGATION Save seeds and sow in spring or transplant self-sown seedlings.

HOUTTUYNIA CORDATA

***Houttuynia cordata* 'Chamaeleon', syn. *H. c.* 'Tricolor'**

Brilliantly colored red, yellow, and green heart-shaped leaves make Houttuynia a popular choice for the pond edge. The white, insignificant flowers are produced in spring. This hardy perennial thrives in wet conditions or shallow water but can become invasive and so should be planted in a container to contain its spread.

- The species *Houttuynia cordata* has red stems, blue-green foliage, and bears single white flowers each pierced by a cone-shaped center.
- *H. c.* 'Flore Pleno' is a double white form.

HEIGHT 6–12 in (15–30 cm)
PLANTING DEPTH To 4 in (10 cm)
PROPAGATION Divide clumps in spring.

***Iris* species**

Various species of iris are suitable for planting in and around the edges of the pond producing an array of lush green foliage and brightly colored flowers in all shades and mixes of white, blue, purple, and red.

- *I. laevigata* is the only species that needs to be grown in the water all the time. It produces its usually blue or white flowers in midsummer and sometimes again in early fall.
- *I. ensata* (Japanese iris) is a large-flowered iris that thrives both in and around the pond.
- *I. pseudacorus* (yellow flag) is attractive, but tends to be much too vigorous for all except the largest garden ponds.
- *I. setosa* bears its light blue or violet flowers in early summer.
- The eye-catching blooms of *I. versicolor* (blue flag) are variously variegated red-purple, green-yellow, and white, but this one does tend to seed rather too freely, and can become a nuisance.

HEIGHT From 18 in–3 ft (45–90 cm)
PLANTING DEPTH To 12 in (30 cm)
PROPAGATION Divide clumps as soon as the flowers fade.

MARGINALS

LOBELIA

Lobelia cardinalis

With purple-red leaves and bright scarlet flowers, this plant is equally at home in a bog garden. It is often attacked by slugs and needs frost protection.

HEIGHT 3 ft (90 cm)
SPREAD 9 in (23 cm)
PLANTING DEPTH 2–3 in (5–7.5 cm)
PROPAGATION By division in spring or cuttings in summer.

Mentha aquatica

Water mint

A useful plant for softening pond edges. The foliage is aromatic when crushed and the whorls of tiny lavender flowers attract bees in summer. Water mint is vigorous, so plant in a basket and trim back stems to control its spread.

HEIGHT 9–12 in (23–30 cm)
PLANTING DEPTH To 3 in (7.5 cm)
PROPAGATION Divide mature plants in spring.

Menyanthes trifoliata

Bog bean

With its sprawling habit, this is a good choice for disguising pond edges. If you are growing it in a small pond, it is a good idea to confine its spread by planting it in a basket. Its dark green leaves resemble broad beans.

HEIGHT 9 in (23 cm)
SPREAD 12 in (30 cm)
PLANTING DEPTH 2-4 in (5-10 cm)
PROPAGATION Divide mature plants in spring.

***Mimulus* species**

Monkey flowers

These yellow, orange, blue or blotched snapdragon-like flowers will brighten up the pond margins in summer. Equally happy in wet conditions or shallow water, they will readily self-seed to produce new plants.

HEIGHT From 12–18 in (30–45 cm)
SPREAD 12 in (30 cm)
PLANTING DEPTH To 5 in (12.5 cm)
PROPAGATION Raise from seed or cuttings taken in summer. Plants can also be divided.

Myosotis scorpioides*, syn. *M. palustris

Water forget-me-not

This is a water-loving version of the popular forget-me-not often seen in flower in gardens in spring. Free-flowering over several weeks from early to midsummer, it will often creep over the edge of the pond to root in the surrounding wet soil. The small bright blue flowers each have a central eye of pink, yellow, or white flowers and are produced in loose clusters. The mid-green leaves are narrow and form sprawling mounds.

HEIGHT 6–9 in (15–23 cm) There is also a shorter growing form.
SPREAD 12 in (30 cm)
PLANTING DEPTH To 3 in (7.5 cm)
PROPAGATION Raise from seed or division.

MIMULUS 'LOTHIAN FIRE'

MARGINALS

PONTEDERIA CORDATA

Pontederia cordata
Pickerel weed
As one of only a handful of blue-flowered marginals, pickerel weed is a popular choice for the edge of a larger pond. A robust, deciduous perennial, it forms dense clumps of stems bearing handsome, narrow heart-shaped leaves, which are smooth and dark green in color. Dense spikes of blue flowers appear from within a leaf at the tip of the stem in late summer.
HEIGHT 30 in (75 cm)
SPREAD 18 in (45 cm)
PLANTING DEPTH 3–6 in (7.5–15 cm)
PROPAGATION Divide in late spring or sow fresh seed.

***Ranunculus lingua* 'Grandiflorus'**
Greater spearwort
Prized for its yellow buttercup flowers, some 2 in (5 cm) in diameter, which are freely produced throughout the summer, this marginal is a vigorous plant only suitable for larger ponds.
• *R. flammula* (lesser spearwort) has smaller flowers and does not grow so tall.
HEIGHT 2–3 ft (60–90 cm)
SPREAD 18 in (45 cm)
PLANTING DEPTH 3–6 in (7.5–15 cm)
PROPAGATION Divide mature plants in spring.

Sagittaria latifolia
American arrowhead, duck potato, wapato
The soft green leaves of this plant resemble arrowheads. Whorls of white flowers appear in summer.
HEIGHT 5 ft (1.5 m)
SPREAD 2 ft (60 cm)
PLANTING DEPTH 6 in (15 cm)
PROPAGATION Divide mature plants in spring.

RANUNCULUS FLAMMULA

Sisyrinchium californicum
Rather like a miniature iris in appearance but with starry bright yellow flowers. An ideal marginal for a smaller pond.
HEIGHT 12–24 in (30–60 cm)
SPREAD 12 in (30 cm)
PLANTING DEPTH To 1 in (2.5 cm)
PROPAGATION Divide in spring.

Typha minima
Dwarf cattail
An elegant plant that forms tufts of slender foliage at the pond's edge. The rust-brown flowers appear in late summer and mature into decorative seed heads.
HEIGHT 2 ft (60 cm)
SPREAD 12 in (30 cm)
PLANTING DEPTH 6 in (15 cm)
PROPAGATION Divide in spring.

Veronica beccabunga
European brooklime
Grown for its pretty dark blue flowers, which have a white eye. Although not evergreen, it retains its trailing foliage for much of the year and can be used to hide the edges of the pond. Cut back as stems become straggly.
HEIGHT 6–9 in (15–23 cm)
PLANTING DEPTH To 4 in (10 cm)
PROPAGATION Take cuttings in summer.

Oxygenators

Although they are not the most attractive or spectacular of all the aquatics, do not underestimate the importance of submerged, or partially submerged, oxygenating plants. Their foliage plays a vital role in keeping the water clear and supplies oxygen and shelter for fish.

OXYGENATORS

Cabomba caroliniana
Fish grass, Washington grass
This is a valuable oxygenator, used by fish for both food and for spawning. The plants form dense spreading hummocks of fan-shaped, coarsely divided bright green leaves. White flowers are borne in summer. It may be cut back by a hard frost. PROPAGATION Take cuttings in summer or divide when dormant.

Callitriche hermaphroditica*, syn. *C. autumnalis
Autumn starwort
Ideal for a shallow pond, this plant produces star-shaped rosettes of leaves on the surface in summer, hence its common name. Under the water, it has masses of light green, cress-like leaves and is one of the few submerged plants that remains active throughout the year. It does, however, need to be kept in check. PROPAGATION Take cuttings in spring or summer.

Ceratophyllum demersum
Hornwort
This oxygenator comes highly recommended, as it will grow in both sun or shade and is easily kept under control as it does not root. Weighted cuttings can be simply dropped into the water. The submerged whorls of dark green, feathery foliage are most attractive. In late fall the stems sink to the bottom and the plant overwinters as dormant buds, producing new stems in spring. This plant provides a popular habitat for aquatic insects. PROPAGATION Take cuttings in spring or summer.

ELEOCHARIS ACICULARIS

Eleocharis acicularis
Needle spike-rush, hair grass
Dense mats of hairlike foliage create an attractive underwater effect. A good oxygenator and hiding place for small aquatic life and also evergreen. PROPAGATION Divide in spring or summer.

Fontinalis antipyretica
Water moss, willow moss
An evergreen, slow-growing plant that thrives in sun or shade and prefers moving to still water. The bunches of branching stems are covered with short, moss-like, dark green leaves. PROPAGATION Divide in spring or summer.

OXYGENATORS

MYRIOPHYLLUM AQUATICUM

Hottonia palustris
Water violet
One of the few flowering oxygenators. The bright green foliage below the surface is finely divided into fernlike leaves, while flower spikes appear in early summer. These rise 6–9 in (15–23 cm) above the water level bearing violetlike flowers, varying in color from white to lilac. The foliage dies down in fall and the plant overwinters as dormant buds. It is not an easy plant to get established, needing still and deep water.
PROPAGATION Take cuttings in summer.

Myriophyllum aquaticum
Water milfoil, Parrot's feather
Long trailing stems carry very fine, feathery, olive-green leaves. A very effective oxygenating plant, it is perfect for a small pond and an ideal habitat for fish spawn.

- *M. spicatum* has bronze-green foliage and also produces red-petaled flowers an inch or so above the water level.

Both these oxygenators need to be kept in check.
PROPAGATION Take cuttings in spring or summer.

Potamogeton crispus
Curled pondweed
Although large-leaved, this oxygenator is fairly restrained and does not usually become invasive, although it will spread rapidly in mud. The long wiry stems bear straplike bronze or green leaves, which are wavy-edged and look rather like seaweed. Insignificant, small crimson and white flowers appear just above the water line in early summer. It prefers moving water to a still pond and will tolerate cloudy or shady water.
PROPAGATION Take stem cuttings in spring or summer.

Ranunculus aquatilis
Water buttercup, crowsfoot
This plant has two leaf types: green and finely divided below the water and clover-shaped on the surface. In early summer, branched stems carry masses of snow-white buttercups with a yellow center either on or a little above the surface. After flowering, the plant dies back. This is a perfect oxygenator for ponds of all sizes as it does not get out of hand, but it can be difficult to establish.
PROPAGATION Take cuttings in spring or summer.

Utricularia vulgaris
Greater bladderwort
This free-floating perennial has feathery, bronze-green, bladderlike leaves that trap aquatic insects. The flowers, which are bright yellow with red-brown streaks and pouched, are held above the water in summer.
PROPAGATION Separate young plantlets in spring or summer.

Vallisneria spiralis
Eelgrass, tape grass
A submerged perennial, with spiraling, strap-shaped, mid-green leaves up to 32 in (80 cm) long. The greenish flowers are produced year round.
PROPAGATION By division in spring or summer.

AROUND THE POND

Many garden plants will thrive in the permanently moist soil around the edges of a pond. Although they are often, somewhat misleadingly, sold as "bog plants," you don't need a bog garden to grow them. Just keep them well watered, particularly in summer.

PLANTS FOR THE PONDSIDE

***Aruncus dioicus* 'Kneiffii'**
Goat's beard
Similar in appearance to an astilbe, only smaller, this variety produces a froth of tiny, star-shaped creamy white flowers from mid- to late summer. The rich green leaves are feathery. Grows well in sun or partial shade. The species *(A. dioicus)* is taller and makes an ideal specimen by a large pond.
HEIGHT 3 ft (90 cm)
SPREAD 20 in (51 cm)
PROPAGATION Divide in spring or fall.

Asplenium scolopendrium
Hart's-tongue fern
An easy-to-grow fern, which produces attractive evergreen, strap-shaped fronds. Once established, it produces spores that develop into young plants. It prefers dappled shade.
• *A. s.* Crispum Group and *A. s.* Marginatum Group look similar but are slightly smaller.
HEIGHT 18–30 in (45–76 cm)
SPREAD 18 in (45 cm)
PROPAGATION Sow spores in summer.

***Astilbe* species**
Always a favorite around the pond, the astilbes have large feathery plumes of white, pink, and red held above deeply cut foliage, which is often coppery in color when it first emerges in spring.
HEIGHT 12–36 in (30–90 cm)
SPREAD 36 in (90 cm)
PROPAGATION Divide, in spring, every two or three years.

GALVANIZED BATHTUB

PLANTS FOR THE PONDSIDE

Cardamine pratensis
Lady's smock, cuckoo flower
This plant's pretty purple, pink, or lilac summer flowers are a rich source of nectar for butterflies. The dark green leaves are composed of up to eight rounded or kidney-shaped leaflets.
HEIGHT 18 in (45 cm)
SPREAD 12 in (30 cm)
PROPAGATION Self-seeds.

Cyperus involucratus
Umbrella grass
This moisture-loving perennial will grow in the shallow margins of a pond or in the waterlogged soil of a bog garden. It thrives in warmer climates. The distinctive leaves are carried on tips of long, arching, slender green stems. In summer, small clusters of greenish brown flowers appear just above the leaves.
HEIGHT 2 ft (60 cm)
PROPAGATION Divide in spring.

Dierama pendulum
Angel's fishing rods
The bell-shaped, pinkish purple flowers are produced at the ends of grasslike leaves in summer.
HEIGHT 3–5 ft (90–150 cm)
SPREAD 6–8 in (15–20 cm)
PROPAGATION Divide in spring.

Filipendula ulmaria
Meadowsweet
A native bog plant with feathery spires of fragrant creamy white flowers in midsummer.
• The fernlike leaves of the variety *F.* 'Aurea' start golden yellow in spring, turning to pale green as the season progresses.
HEIGHT 1–3 ft (30–90 cm)
SPREAD 12 in (30 cm)
PROPAGATION Divide large clumps in spring or fall.

Gunnera manicata
Giant rhubarb
This impressively sized plant is only suitable for larger water gardens. In summer it produces a bizarre, conelike flower spike, 3-plus ft (90-plus cm) high. In winter the crown will need protecting from frost, so cover it with straw or bracken.
HEIGHT 5–8 ft (1.5–2.4 m)
SPREAD 7 ft (2.1 m)
PROPAGATION Divide crowns in early spring.

***Hemerocallis* species**
Daylily
Although each individual lilylike flower only lasts a day, most daylilies produce their trumpet-shaped flowers in succession over a period of up to six weeks in the summer. Modern hybrids, with their long, straplike leaves, come in a range of vibrant colors from bright yellow and orange to pink and maroon. The flowers have a delicate appearance and may have colored streaks or bands on the petals. They thrive best in a sunny location.
HEIGHT 2–3 ft (60–90 cm)
SPREAD 2–3 ft (60–90 cm)
PROPAGATION Divide clumps in spring or fall.

HEMEROCALLIS

6

PLANTS FOR THE PONDSIDE

***Hosta* species**
Plantain lilies
A group of handsome, shade and moisture-loving foliage plants. Many hostas produce arching spikes of white or lavender-blue flowers above distinctly colored leaves. Their main drawback is that slugs and snails find them irresistible, but a mulch of sharp gravel should help keep these pests at bay.
HEIGHT More than 18 in (45 cm)
SPREAD 1–3 ft (30–90 cm)
PROPAGATION Divide in spring.

Iris siberica
With their dense clumps of slender leaves topped with a mass of dainty flowers in early summer, the Siberian hybrids are a must for pondsides. The flowers are blue, white, and yellow, some attractively veined red.
HEIGHT More than 18 in (45 cm)
PROPAGATION Divide after flowering.

***Lysimachia nummularia* 'Aurea'**
This golden-yellow-leaved variety of creeping Jenny, will quickly spread to carpet a large area. Bright yellow flowers appear in summer.
HEIGHT 1–2 in (2.5–5 cm)
PROPAGATION Divide in spring or fall.

Lythrum salicaria
Purple loosestrife
Narrow spires of closely packed purple-red flowers add interest around the pond. Shorter hybrids are available in various shades of red
HEIGHT 2–4 ft (60–120 cm)
SPREAD 18 in (45 cm)
PROPAGATION Divide clumps in fall.

Matteuccia struthiopteris
Ostrich-feather, shuttlecock fern
A beautiful and hardy fern for the pondside, with its green and feathery fronds arranged like a shuttlecock.
HEIGHT 2 ft (60 cm)
SPREAD 18 in (45 cm)
PROPAGATION Divide crown in spring.

Osmunda regalis
Royal fern
This impressive fern grows particularly well by the water, but, owing to its size, it does need growing space and will suit a large pondside. The bright green fronds, which are pinkish when young, turn bronze in fall. In summer, pale brown flower spikes appear at the tops of the taller fronds. Cover the crown with straw or dead leaves over winter.
HEIGHT More than 4–6 ft (1.2–1.8 m)
SPREAD 3 ft (90 cm)
PROPAGATION Divide crown in spring.

LYSIMACHIA CILIATA

PLANTS FOR THE PONDSIDE

Darmera peltata*, syn. *Peltiphyllum peltatum
Umbrella plant, Indian rhubarb
Clusters of striking white or pale pink flowers on white-haired stems appear in spring before the umbrella-like leaves unfurl.
HEIGHT 3 ft (90 cm)
SPREAD 2 ft (60 cm)
PROPAGATION Divide crown in spring.

***Rheum palmatum* 'Rubrum'**
Ornamental rhubarb
Grown as a specimen plant by the pond, this variety of rhubarb is hardy and will tolerate sun or light shade. Its handsome leaves, flushed dark red, can spread 6 ft (1.8 m) or more, so only grow it there is plenty of room at your pondside.
HEIGHT 8–10 ft (2.4–3 m)
PROPAGATION Divide crown in spring.

Rodgersia pinnata
Sprays of numerous small starry flowers, ranging from yellowish white through to pink and red, are produced in summer. The dark green leaves are crinkled, heavily veined, and glossy. handsome foliage in summer.
HEIGHT 2–3 ft (60–90 cm)
SPREAD 2 ft (60 cm)
PROPAGATION Divide clumps in spring or fall.

Schizostylis coccinea
Kaffir lily
This attractive plant is a useful addition around the pond as the spikes of crimson, red, and pink flowers are produced in abundance in late summer into fall. The leaves are upright, narrow and swordlike, with distinct midribs.
HEIGHT 2–3 ft (60–90 cm)
SPREAD 12 in (30 cm)
PROPAGATION Divide in spring.

***Tradescantia x andersoniana* 'Bilberry Ice'**
Spiderwort
Like other varieties in the Andersoniana Group, 'Bilberry Ice' is clump-forming perennial with long, narrow, fleshy, green leaves, which are occasionally purple-tinted. 'Bilberry Ice' has white and blue-streaked flowers in summer.
HEIGHT More than 2 ft (60 cm)
SPREAD 18 in (45 cm)
PROPAGATION Increase by division in the fall.

Trollius europaeus
Globeflower
The globular, buttercup-like flowers appear in late spring to early summer. The leaves are divided into toothed leaflets.
HEIGHT Over 2 ft (60 cm)
SPREAD 18 in (45 cm)
PROPAGATION Divide in the fall, every three years.

TRADESCANTIA 'BILBERRY ICE'

INDEX

ACKNOWLEDGEMENTS

p. 11 Steven Wooster/designer Michael Balston; p. 13 Steven Wooster/designer Geofrrey Whiten; p. 14 Clive Nichols/designer Julian Treyer-Evans; p. 15 Andrew Lawson; p. 18 Steven Wooster/Chris Gregory; p. 19 Steven Wooster/designer Myles Challis; p. 37 Andrew Lawson; p. 61 Steven Wooster/designer Michael Balston; p. 76 Andrew Lawson/Marwood Hill, Devon; p. 77 Andrew Lawson; p. 78 John Glover; p. 91 Andrew Lawson; p. 100 Andrew Lawson; p. 101 S&O Mathews; p. 102 Clive Nichols. Thanks to Tim Stansfield; Country Gardens, Tring; Jane Haley-Pursey and staff at Solesbridge Mill Water Gardens, Chorleywood; Spear and Jackson.